Enlightenment is a Secret

TEACHINGS OF
LIBERATION

Andrew Cohen

MOKSHA PRESS

1995

OTHER BOOKS BY ANDREW COHEN

An Unconditional Relationship to Life
Autobiography of an Awakening
My Master Is My Self

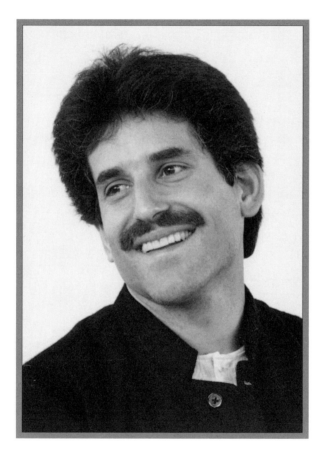

Contents

Acknowledgements

I want to thank Chris Parish for his help in overseeing the transcription of the material; Judith Fox for her help with design, production and her continual support; Steve Brett and Amy Edelstein for their help in selecting and organizing the material; Kathy Bayer for all of her assistance in helping to see this book to its completion. And most of all I want to thank Bradley Roth for all the work he put into this project. I want to thank him especially for his constant encouragement and unending support and inspiration without which this book would never have happened.

Foreword

Nine years ago Andrew Cohen came into my life like a thunderbolt and instantly my life caught fire. Even though I had been on the spiritual path for a long time, meeting him was something I could not ever have been prepared for. In one moment, as we sat together in his room on a sparkling November afternoon, everything that I thought I knew, the entire fabric of my known universe, exploded in the recognition of my own true nature. I knew without any doubt that my search was at an end, and yet I was soon to discover that an extraordinary life had only just begun.

Andrew Cohen is that rare phenomenon in any age, a truly enlightened human being and a real teacher of Liberation. As a result of his powerful awakening and complete surrender to the Truth in 1986, his own life since that day has been an expression of what is possible for anyone who truly wants to be free. Grounded irrevocably in that unknown mystery at the core of Life itself, yet soaring freely, guided only by a singular passion for the Truth, he is an evolutionary fire, a catalyst in this world of time and space for revolutionary transformation.

From the moment Andrew began to teach nine years ago he immediately had an extraordinary impact on those around him, exactly as he had on me. His constant message that Enlightenment is utterly realizable right here and now and the absolute authenticity of his condition carried a transmission which was electrifying and spoke straight to the heart. Many, many people who came to see him had explosive, spontaneous realizations of the undivided nature of Life which were to alter the entire course and foundation of their lives. As word of these miraculous events spread far and wide many began to gather around Andrew in an ecstatic and magical atmosphere of boundless freedom and Self-discovery. At the same time Andrew's absolute and uncompromising relationship to the Truth and his passion in questioning everything to that end, including many of the spiritual paradigms of the time, from the very beginning gave him a controversial reputation in the spiritual world.

After some months passed however, it became clear to Andrew that in spite of the fact that so many people around him had experienced a similar revelation to that which had completely transformed his own life, it hadn't succeeded in permanently liberating them in the same way. The real foundation of Andrew's teaching began in his discovery that even an explosive experience of the Absolute was not enough to liberate an individual from the power of their own conditioning as long as they remained divided to any degree about their desire to be free. Indeed this, he discovered, was the condition of most seekers. The question of the fundamental intention of the individual in relationship to absolute transformation was to become the foundation, the cornerstone of his teaching.

Independent of any spiritual tradition, guided solely by his own recognition and passion for the Truth and his ever-deepening understanding of the human condition, Andrew began to uncover the fundamental principles that lie at the heart of the spiritual endeavor. In time, a fully comprehensive spiritual teaching began to emerge, which could clearly and unambiguously convey to the serious seeker both the Goal and the Way.

Enlightenment Is a Secret consists of excerpts from teachings Andrew gave between the years 1986 and 1990, which have all been finally selected, arranged and edited by Andrew himself. In the hands of anyone open to be touched by the Unknown, *Enlightenment Is a Secret* brings us immediately to the very edge of our understanding, opening up a boundless vista before us. Since its publication in 1991, this flawless and unadorned transmission of the enlightened vision has awakened in thousands of seekers across the world an immediate recognition of that perspective that often remains as only the shadowy intimation of an unthinkable possibility. Every page of this remarkable book reverberates with a transcendent emptiness. Every word echoes the sacred Mystery out of which it was conceived. Stripped away from the familiar reference points of spiritual tradition, time and practice, its utterly authentic and deeply penetrating expression of liberated understanding plunges the reader into a direct contemplation of the possibility of Liberation here and now, evoking in an open heart the whispering of a deep knowing beyond the mind.

Absolutely mystical in nature, *Enlightenment Is a Secret* is simultaneously utterly pragmatic, illuminating with astonishing clarity a subject that for many has been safely shrouded in mystery and superstition. Like no other book I have read, *Enlightenment Is a Secret* is an exact and complete guide through the perilous territory of the spiritual journey. It addresses with extraordinary insight and in a vast and impersonal context, all of the essential aspects of spiritual life. It is in fact a blueprint of Awakening, of Goal and Path, constantly meeting in very real terms the dichotomy between our enlightened potential and the complex and divided nature of our very human condition.

This is not an easy teaching to keep a safe distance from. It meets the spiritual seeker head on, immediately bringing us face to face with exactly where we stand, here and now, in relationship to the possibility of *going all the way*. Andrew challenges us to come to a clear and final resolution about our desire to be Free, pointing out that it is not spiritual experiences in themselves that have the power to truly liberate us, but only the degree to which we are willing to respond, in every aspect of our lives, to the implications inherent in them. Andrew confronts us throughout the course of the book with the absolute nature of the spiritual quest and the tremendous sacrifice involved, revealing the utterly volitional nature of the division within ourselves that too often allows us to fall short of that perfect death he is calling us to. Supremely challenging, this rare compilation of excerpts demystifies what has always been involved in true awakening, putting the responsibility for our own Liberation entirely on our willingness to truly change. Andrew's teaching points to the goal as being not merely an inner perspective, but the total transformation of our human life, an event which has profound evolutionary significance for humanity as a whole.

Dare to let this book penetrate your heart. Its explosive and liberating call to awaken has the power to set you Free.

Steve Brett

Preface

Enlightenment is a secret. I began teaching in 1986 and have met thousands of people. Since that time I have been surprised to discover how few people seem to know anything about this secret. Many speak about it, and in recent times many have written about it, but very few, I continue to discover, truly know anything about it. Contemplation and direct Realization of the Absolute is the most demanding and all-consuming form of meditation that a human being can pursue. It is so dangerous, because of the perfectly immaculate nature of the Absolute Realization. Any trace of self-interest of any kind in any form instantly corrupts that most perfect purity and automatically, although usually imperceptibly, taints its reflection. How to Realize everything and remain untouched even by that? How difficult it is to remain free from all the temptations that direct Realization invites. Even those who do know and have Realized usually allow themselves to stop far short of that immaculate and perfect death that casts no reflection and recognizes only itself. Why is it so difficult to Realize everything, to accumulate nothing and stand absolutely alone? It is out of that aloneness that this book was created.

Andrew Cohen
August 16, 1991

It's a very scary thing to say, "I want to be Free."
It can be very terrifying. It means that the ground from
under you can fall away at any moment. When you say,
"I want to be Free," and mean it, it's the same as saying,
"I'm ready to die." It is a voluntary choice of death
while you're still alive. It changes everything. It's just
like committing suicide, because you are making a
conscious choice.

I remember — in my case, I had been with my teacher
for two weeks, and we were sitting quietly in his room
when I said out loud, "I'm ready to die but I don't know
how." This was a shock to me — I jumped. It just came out
by itself. I realized I hadn't been thinking about it. I said
again, "I'm ready to die but I don't know how." This was
a real declaration of death. It meant that I was ready to
give up this life for another. Maybe you will be terrified.
I was scared at the time, but it didn't stop me.

Enlightenment

The Real Contentment

The conscious realization of perfect happiness is the bliss of Nirvana.

Coming to Rest

Q: I'd like to understand what Enlightenment is.

A: It is relief. It is cessation. It is the end of becoming. It's the end of the struggle to become anyone or anything. It's coming finally to rest, here and now, in this life.

Enlightenment Is Not Far Away

Enlightenment is *not* far away. It does *not* need to take time. As long as you insist that it must take time, then you are still interested in protecting yourself. If you are still interested in protecting yourself, then it means that you are not interested in that which is beyond the mind. If you truly want to be Free you have to give up, you have to just give up. You have to give up completely.

Enlightenment Is a Secret

Enlightenment is a secret that very few people know about and even fewer understand. Why is it a secret? Because Enlightenment does not exist in time. That's why it's a secret and that's why it will always be a secret. Enlightenment is a vision that cannot be held or grasped in any way. Beyond this world it's a mystery that is exploding. A fire that is burning. It's a fire that a person is either going to jump into or run away from. This fire burns beyond the mind. No-time is the place where this secret abides. Realize that and you realize the Self you are when there's no mind and no time. Realize that, and cling to that alone as your own Self.

Longing for Liberation

The Possibility

You Have to Get Out of the Way

The Impossible Possibility

Precious Vulnerability

That Most Delicate Place

Be Ready to Receive the Real

You Have to Get Out of the Way

There is a secret that is infinitely greater than anything you have ever known. It is real and it exists and if you make room for it—it will overwhelm you.

You have to get out of the way. You have to abandon everything you've been taught and everything you've been led to believe —all those limiting, confining, imprisoning, denying ideas and concepts that you have picked up along your way. You have to make room for that which is unbelievable. You have to get out of the way. "Oh my God!" you'll say, "I didn't know it could be like this."

The Impossible Possibility

If you want to be Free you have to open yourself up to that unthinkable possibility, that impossible possibility. You have to allow yourself to consider that which is immeasurable. You have to rise up. You have to open your mind, open your heart, and renounce the past completely.

Precious Vulnerability

When there is a suspension of all cherished beliefs and memories, there is a precious vulnerability that most people don't allow themselves to recognize. What is this precious vulnerability? It is allowing oneself to consider the possibility of Freedom.

That moment is very precious. Most people squander it. They don't realize how precious it really is.

That Most Delicate Place

There is a place in all of us that has remained inno-cent, uncorrupted and untouched by the world. We have to locate that most delicate place. It is a very sensitive place, it's where we feel love — where tenderness and compassion arise, free from self-interest.

This place is the hole we have to fall into — and disappear in forever.

Be Ready to Receive the Real

The real is always looking for you. Be ready to receive it. Be ready for that unexpected tap on your shoulder. If you're not ready you will miss it, and a chance such as this does not come twice in a lifetime. The real does not wait for you, the real does not wait for the unreal. Don't wait. Be ready for that which cannot be imagined. Be ready to give your heart forever.

Longing for Liberation

Where Is Your Passion?

Wanting to Realize More Than Anything Else

Be Obedient to the Longing

Is It Possible to Desire Freedom Too Much?

Where Is Your Passion?

Where is your passion for Liberation? Without passion for Liberation there is no hope for Liberation. Passion for Liberation *is* your Liberation, and if you surrender to that passion and become a slave of that passion, your fate will be sealed. But if for any reason that passion gets burned out, then it won't happen this time around. Realize it has only to do with you. It's always up to you alone. Do not allow yourself to stop until you are sure that there is nothing more to realize and nothing more to know.

Go to the absolute limit. If you want it all to change you simply have to realize *you* are the solution. That's what Liberation is. That's why I said, "Where is your passion?"

Wanting to Realize
More Than Anything Else

Wanting to Realize — that's the crux, the key issue. Truly wanting that more than anything else and knowing you want it more than anything else. Grace cannot function uninhibitedly unless in your heart of hearts, Realization is all that you want. If you are serious it's got to be choiceless.

Be Obedient to the Longing

Q: How can I deepen my longing for Liberation?

A: By being obedient to it. You must be obedient to that longing above all others. Always put that longing first — then you will be successful. That longing will surely lead you home, but not necessarily in the way that you have in mind. That cannot be known beforehand. Most people accumulate too many ideas about what is going to happen and how it is going to happen. In this, they are following only their mind, lost in imagination.

Real longing for Liberation is something that burns. In that burning there is no mind, there is no age, there is no face and there is no history — there is only that longing. Force yourself to be obedient to that longing. If you cannot, then you will surely start looking in other places, because you will want to find some security in this very miserable world. Be vigilant. Be obedient to that longing alone.

Is It Possible to Desire Freedom Too Much?

Q: Is it possible to desire Freedom too much? Couldn't the eagerness in me be an obstacle?

A: Wanting to be truly Free is the most demanding task a human being can ever undertake. Do you know why? Because anything else you could ever want and may decide to pursue can only be something that you are *doing*. In that there will always be some separation between what you are doing and who and what you are. In true Enlightenment, that separation cannot exist any longer. I am speaking about a condition that is a permanent endeavor, a permanent preoccupation. Nothing could be more demanding. It's not possible to want to be Free too much. Because if you want to be Free it will take everything that you have to give.

How could wanting Freedom too much ever be a hindrance? You have to want it that much for there to be any real chance that you will succeed.

Clarity of Intention

Clarity of Intention:
The Foundation of Spiritual Life

What Do I Really Want?

In This Birth

The Choices Are the Known and the Unknown

Waking Up Is Not a Game

Clarity of Intention:
The Foundation of Spiritual Life

The foundation of spiritual life is clarity of intention. Do I really want to be Free, here and now? You have to decide, do I want to be Free? Once the intention is clear, the mind becomes focused. When the mind is focused there is one-pointedness. When there is one-pointedness, the Heart will guide you. It will indicate what needs to be left behind and what needs to be avoided.

Clarity of intention reveals the Heart. When the Heart is revealed trust is found and intuition flowers. Then one starts to understand what it means to live in the unknown. Then you can know what it is to be blind, and see everywhere.

What Do I Really Want?

"What is my intention?" means what do I *really* want? Do I want to be Free? Do I *really* want to be Free? Am I willing to sacrifice for that Freedom? If so, how much am I willing to sacrifice for that Freedom? How much am I willing to give up? How much pain am I willing to cease to be preoccupied with? How many ideas am I willing to part with? How many ideas about Enlightenment am I willing to let go of?

Looking seriously into questions like these reveals the clarity or lack of clarity of your intention.

In This Birth

You have to have the clear intention that you want to be Free. In this birth. In this lifetime, this time around. *Now* — not at any time in the future, but right *now*. This is what you have to want, and you have to mean it, and you have to be willing to stake your life on it. It means there's nothing that's more important to you than Liberation.

If you're that serious and that one-pointed about it, you can't fail.

The Choices Are the Known
and the Unknown

Q: It seems that in coming to clarity of intention, one should be clear about what the choices are.

A: The choices are the known and the unknown. There are no other choices. The unknown includes everything and excludes nothing, but the known excludes quite a bit. The known means time and space, thought and memory. The unknown is much more than that. It means without limits.

Q: This frightens me. It makes me feel lonely and powerless.

A: If you are lucky you will find yourself utterly power-less and at the mercy of precisely what you are afraid of.

Q: Is there a specific way to deal with this fear?

A: Yes. Clarity of intention. This means being absolutely clear and utterly doubtless about wanting to be Free here and now in this very birth. That means being ready right now, come what may.

Waking Up Is Not a Game

Q: How does one practice clarity of intention?

A: Simply ask yourself, "What do I really want? Am I ready and willing to be Free, here and now?"

Q: I don't feel ready yet, I still feel bound in time. What kind of practice should I do to ripen my readiness?

A: You should ask yourself, "*Why* don't I feel ready right now?! What is it I'm afraid of? What is it I'm unwilling to let go of? What is it that's holding me back from letting go of everything I've ever known?"

Q: That's a supremely direct path.

A: Waking up is not a game. That's why you have to be deadly serious about this. There is tremendous sacrifice involved and if you're not ready to struggle and face your worst fears then you have no business seeking for Enlightenment in the first place. A serious person can't bear to wait any longer. A person who is not serious feels that they have all the time in the world.

Be Deadly Serious

Be Deadly Serious

People Who Are Serious Succeed

The Ego Never Sought Enlightenment

What Does It Mean to Be Serious about
Awakening?

Be Deadly Serious

There is a difference between being serious and being deadly serious. When you are deadly serious you do not have any time to waste, and this makes your relationship with the Truth very different from when you are just serious. When you are serious you have time, but when you are deadly serious you do not have any time at all.

People Who Are Serious Succeed

People who are serious succeed; people who are not serious do not succeed.

If you want to succeed, you have to make sure you do. It's up to you. If you make sure you do, then you will. And if you're deadly serious, nobody will be able to stop you.

The Ego Never Sought Enlightenment

A: You have to be deadly serious about being deadly serious. When you are deadly serious about being deadly serious, you will soon find that the ego never sought Enlightenment. You will discover that the ego could never ever want to be Enlightened. Realize that. Realize that the ego never wanted anything to do with it.

When you realize that it is not the ego that seeks Enlightenment you will stumble upon the Heart and find what you have been looking for all along.

Q: Is being deadly serious a matter of choice?

A: Ignorant people always have a choice. Deadly serious people never do.

What Does It Mean to Be Serious about Awakening?

Q: What does it mean to be serious about Awakening?

A: To be serious about Awakening means you have finally come to the end of the line.

Q: What does that mean?

A: To be serious about Awakening means an individual has come to that point in their evolution when they are finally, once and for all willing, ready, and profoundly interested in taking full responsibility for what it means to be a fully human being.

Only then can karma finally come to an end.

What Does It Mean to Be Ready?

What Qualities Insure the Likelihood of Success?

Readiness for Enlightenment Is True Innocence

What Qualities Insure
the Likelihood of Success?

Q: What qualities would insure the likelihood of success for a sincere seeker in their search for Enlightenment?

A: To carry the jewel of Enlightenment successfully you must have a lot of courage. You must be humble and not proud. You must have true integrity. You should mean what you say and say what you mean. You should be able to express your intentions honestly and be able to follow through on them. Also there must be correlation between your words and deeds.

It is important to be able to consistently manifest these virtues. Without consistency then honesty, humility, integrity and courage have no meaning or value. Without consistency in these virtues it will be impossible for any human being to carry the jewel of Enlightenment successfully.

Readiness for Enlightenment
Is True Innocence

Q: What does it mean to be ready for Enlightenment?

A: People are in different states of readiness and readiness for Enlightenment is true innocence. If there is true innocence it means that the ego will not be a big obstruction to Liberation. We are born with this innocence and it is this very innocence in us that experiences the pain of separation.

The awakening of Self-recognition is when this innocence recognizes itself as the Self and ego is recognized as non-Self. Under the weight of this Self-discovery the ego is seen as unreal. This is when the whole universe turns upside down and this is when all is revealed to be very different than it had seemed.

Q: This frightens me.

A: Ego is the illusion of separateness that doesn't want to give up its illusion of separateness. Remember it is not the ego that longs to be Free.

Who Is a Teacher?

The Teacher Is an Outward Manifestation
of Your Own Heart

A Perfect Mirror

What Does It Mean to Be Perfect?

The Teacher Is an Outward
Manifestation of Your Own Heart

Some people feel a yearning and a burning that is a kind of quiet agony. This is when it becomes painfully obvious that something absolutely fundamental to our very existence is unresolved, incomplete and unsatisfied. Some begin to seek, pray, read and meditate to try and satisfy this yearning and bring this pain to an end.

When you find a real Teacher there is a movement that is most precious, very delicate and inconceivably sacred. The Teacher is an outward manifestation of your own heart, and responds only to that pull which is already there within you. Like two lovers, the attraction can become unbearable.

When the yearning within you and the open heart of a real Teacher come together, it is a very delicate moment.

A Perfect Mirror

Q: What is the function of a spiritual Teacher?

A: The function of a spiritual Teacher is to serve as a perfect mirror for the student. A spiritual Teacher should be a mirror that is immaculate and completely unstained. There should not be even one speck of dust on that mirror, so in that mirror the student will be able to see their own reflection perfectly and absolutely clearly.

What Does It Mean to Be Perfect?

Q: If a spiritual Teacher claims to be Enlightened, I expect him or her to be perfect.

A: A supposedly Enlightened Teacher should be perfect. But what does it mean to be perfect? What is perfection all about? What does it mean to not only have entered the stream but to have drowned in the stream? That's something that one has to go into. You have to find that out for yourself. But once you do find out, the life of your Teacher should represent that which you have discovered.

Seeking

Abandon Every Idea

Abandon Every Idea about Enlightenment

No Idea

God Is Not an Object to Be Seen

Don't Be Satisfied with Imitation

Abandon Every Idea about Enlightenment

In order to be successful in your quest for Freedom, it is imperative that you unconditionally abandon every idea that you have about Enlightenment. As long as you think that Enlightenment is something that can be understood by the mind, the cycle of blindly perpetuating your own ignorance will never cease.

No Idea

Q: Would this be an accurate description of Enlightenment: accepting the whole universe as yourself and loving the universe as yourself?

A: No, it would not. Having no idea about the universe and having no idea about yourself. *That* would be more like it.

God Is Not an Object to Be Seen

The individual who is deluded tries to know that which is unimaginable with his mind. In his delusion he sees God as an object. In his delusion he is looking outside himself, waiting for God to appear before him. He hasn't understood. He hasn't understood that God is not an object to be seen. Few people ever understand this.

Most people carry around pictures of reality in their minds. It is only when all pictures of reality have truly been abandoned that something unimaginable can happen.

Don't Be Satisfied with Imitation

Don't be satisfied with imitation. If the Dharma has been Realized, it actually becomes what you are. Don't allow yourself to be satisfied with merely trying to conform to an idea of what you believe the Truth to be. You have to have the courage and conviction to give up absolutely every idea that you have about what the Truth is and be willing to make the effort to find out what the Truth is for yourself.

You have to have the kind of determination and independent spirit that will enable you to become, without any hesitation, that which you have Realized.

Seek Until You Find

Seek Until You Find

Start Again

When You Realize You Don't Know Anything
It Will Be Very Easy to Let Go

Lost Innocence

Seek Until You Find

You must seek until you find. Only when you find what you have been looking for will you be able to truly stop seeking. Better not to stop seeking energetically until then. It is imperative that you do not stop seeking until you reach the goal of perfect Enlightenment. Do not allow yourself to stop until you've come to the absolute end of all seeking. Only when you have come home forever and you know without any doubt that it is all over should you allow yourself to stop.

Start Again

Seek with a renewed vigor and a renewed spirit, without all the disillusionment of your past. Begin once again, throwing away all the conclusions that you have reached from all the experiences that you have had. Start again, fresh, with renewed innocence. Begin once again, knowing nothing, like a beginner.

You are either a seeker or a finder. Many people claim they have stopped seeking even though they clearly haven't found what they were originally looking for. They say this because they have been on the path for a very long time. Many have come to all the correct conclusions, but only intellectually. The real event has not yet taken place. Without realizing it, they are completely lost.

If you are a finder you will know it, and you won't have any doubt about it. So unless this is the case, continue to seek. And seek until you find, forgetting everything that you thought you knew before.

When You Realize You Don't Know Anything It Will Be Very Easy to Let Go

Q: I have been seeking for a very long time. I've spent time with different teachers, I've practiced several different methods of meditation and I've read many spiritual books. In spite of all that, I'm not Enlightened and I'm still seeking. Because I have learned so much from all I have done, sometimes I think I know what Enlightenment is when I actually don't.

A: In the beginning something compelled you to seek. Then you sought out books and teachers and like-minded people, but you didn't find what you were looking for. Along the way you have accumulated everything except that which you were originally seeking for, which was Liberation. You have accumulated so much and what you wanted was only to be free from all accumulation. In fact, you have only burdened yourself.

Once you truly realize and accept the fact that you actually don't know anything about Enlightenment, it will be very easy to let go. But as long as you have even a small belief in the idea that you really do understand, you will miss it. If you deeply and profoundly recognize that you are completely ignorant on the subject of

Enlightenment, then it will be very easy for you to let go of all that you have acquired, become attached to and are now imprisoned by.

Lost Innocence

Q: When I started my spiritual search I felt a great deal of joy, excitement and wonder. It was like I was on a honeymoon, but it didn't last very long. Since that time my search has been motivated only by the memory of this honeymoon.

A: Often when people begin their search there is a rediscovery of a lost innocence. It is the realization of this innocence that is the door to the profound happiness that many people are looking for. In their initial spiritual experiences many discover that they are on a mysterious adventure that seems limitless and potentially without end. This is very thrilling. What allowed this innocence to surface is that they began to question everything that they had until that moment believed to be true. They suddenly realized that they had lived most of their lives with a profoundly limited perspective. They discovered that they actually had no understanding of the way things truly are. All was brought into question in the immensity revealed to them in their initial experiences.

This newfound innocence, which is so thrilling and such a source of inspiration, usually lasts only a short time. This is because there is a profound vulnerability that always accompanies this innocence and this vulnerability is usually too much for most people to bear. In order to escape this vulnerability many doubt its ultimate validity or else take pride in their spiritual accomplishment. In this way, the innocence and purity is lost. Without even realizing it, the potential for profound transformation slips through their fingers. This happens only because they cannot bear the unbearable vulnerability and emptiness of knowing absolutely nothing.

Spiritual Practice

Spiritual Is What You Already Are

You Cannot Prepare for Where You Already Are

Is It Necessary to Meditate in Order to Reach
Enlightenment?

Don't Want Time to Understand

The True Path

Are You Going to Jump or Not?

Oil and Water Do Not Mix

What Kind of Practice Can Prepare One
for Enlightenment?

Enlightenment Is Where All Practice Is
Supposed to Lead

Devotion Cannot Be Practiced

Spiritual Progress

Spiritual Is What You Already Are

When many people think about the spiritual life what comes to their mind is a life of performing various religious functions like worship, prayer, meditation, singing, dancing and reading. When someone does these things very sincerely many think that makes them spiritual. None of that necessarily has anything to do with what spiritual truly is. Spiritual is the very nature of what you already are. There's nothing to do about it except to Realize it. Once you have made this discovery it's all over. Then there is literally nothing more to do. When I realized this, it shocked me for days.

You Cannot Prepare for Where You Already Are

There is nothing to overcome and nothing to prepare for — you cannot prepare for where you already are.

If you believe that some process in time will gradually release you from the illusion of samsara, then you are in a very secure position. But if you realize that the idea of time *is* the illusion of samsara then the whole business is finished up very quickly. As long as there is any investment in the future, you are a hundred billion miles away from home.

Is It Necessary to Meditate in Order to Reach Enlightenment?

Q: Is it necessary to meditate in order to reach Enlightenment?

A: It is necessary to destroy the obstacles to meditation if you are to be Enlightened.

Q: How can I destroy all the obstacles to meditation? Is there any technique that can help me to do that?

A: If meditation is to be effortless then you cannot have a mind burdened by guilt, doubt, suspicion, superstition, resentment or fear. Destroy all the obstacles to meditation and Enlightenment will be yours.

Don't Want Time to Understand

Q: I want some kind of method.

A: There is no method. The only method is the truth itself. Wake up and see it. That *is* the method. Why do you want a method? Method means: time to understand. That is the problem. Do you want to understand? Then don't want time to understand. Then everything will be different.

If the pure intention is there and you want to understand, then don't want time to understand.

The True Path

Q: What is the true path?

A: The true path is whatever gets you there. The true path is whatever actually sets you Free. That means whatever path that is successful in *this* life. "In this life" means *now*. That which you can realize the success of in *this* moment.

The true path is that path which is perfectly successful.

Are You Going to Jump or Not?

Q: Do you recommend any practices that help bring one to the ultimate goal of Enlightenment?

A: The practice of Enlightenment is the end in itself. A lot of practices are supposed to bring you to Enlightenment. Some spiritual practices can bring you to the very edge of the known. But the question is, when you are at the very edge of everything you have ever thought or imagined—what are you going to do? Are you going to jump or not? That is the only relevant question. Many people have had profound spiritual experiences and have come very close; very, very close to the edge. But when they were overcome by a tremendous fear they went back. They withdrew. What are *you* going to do? Are you going to jump? Are you ready to die? Are you interested? Is that what you want right now? If the answer is no, then you are not interested in Enlightenment. If the answer is yes, then it is going to happen.

Oil and Water Do Not Mix

Sadhana means time. Enlightenment is the destruction of time. Like oil and water, Enlightenment and time do not mix. When you realize that Freedom has no history you will laugh and it will all be over.

What Kind of Practice Can Prepare One for Enlightenment?

Q: What kind of practice can prepare one for Enlightenment?

A: Spiritual practice is not necessarily a preparation for Enlightenment. The only true preparation for Enlightenment is humility. A humble person, who is truly sincere, is fully prepared. Spiritual practice does not necessarily lead to humility.

Enlightenment Is Where
All Practice Is Supposed to Lead

Q: Does waking up necessarily involve a discipline or
a practice?

A: Freedom only has to do with understanding. Always
attached to a discipline or a practice is a large investment
in the future. Any investment in the future is the very
foundation of ignorance. The future always implies time
and waking up means the realization of the end of time.

Q: I have a spiritual practice and when I do it I experience some understanding. Are you saying it's useless?

A: What I'm saying is that Enlightenment is where all
your practice is supposed to be leading. I'm saying realize
that goal immediately. That *is* understanding. Then you
will be released from the terrible burden of becoming —
and that is Peace.

Q: What then is meditation?

A: When you have recognized the truth of who you
really are an explosion takes place. Suddenly the whole
question of becoming is finished. The duality of bondage

versus liberation, samsara versus nirvana, no longer applies. That is when you discover what meditation is. When you are no longer concerned with overcoming anything or realizing anything, then meditation is spontaneous and effortless.

Devotion Cannot Be Practiced

Q: Can devotion be practiced?

A: Devotion is not something that can be practiced. Devotion is a choiceless response to Self-recognition that is imposed from within. Devotion is imposed from the unknown upon the ego and this cannot be practiced. It can only be experienced. The practice of devotion is an attempt by the ego through effort to impose itself upon the unknown. This cannot be done.

Devotion is an imposition from the unknown upon the ego that is an agonizingly ecstatic and excruciatingly vulnerable spiritual experience.

Spiritual Progress

Q: Is there such a thing as spiritual progress?

A: As long as there is any trace of ignorance left, there certainly is. But when every trace of ignorance has been destroyed, progress comes to an end. Progress itself is part of the illusion, even though it seems real. "Something has happened, I'm changing, I'm going somewhere, something is happening to me."

Finally one realizes that nothing happened, ever. You realize that all the drama of life was only a dream. Even the waking up.

Relationship with a Teacher

What Makes for a Successful Student-Teacher
Relationship?

A Perfect Relationship to Life

The Teacher and Liberation Should Be
One and the Same

In the Beginning It's Up to the Teacher

A Secret Relationship

What Makes for a Successful
Student-Teacher Relationship?

Q: What makes for a successful student-teacher relationship?

A: A worthy student and a worthy teacher. A seeker who is truly earnest and a teacher who is fully Realized. Clarity of intention in both parties and equally full acceptance of responsibility. If both teacher and student are sincere, earnest and fully responsible, then it need not take much time at all. As long as the commitment to Liberation is total, the outcome is assured.

A Perfect Relationship to Life

Q: I'm confused about the difference between surrendering to myself and surrendering to a Teacher.

A: Surrendering to yourself and surrendering to the Teacher should be the same thing. The relationship with the Teacher should be synonymous with a perfect relationship to life, to reality, and to yourself. This relationship implies far more than being involved with another personality. Very few people understand this.

The Teacher and Liberation Should Be One and the Same

The Teacher and Liberation should be one and the same thing. The relationship to the Teacher should be such that that relationship could only liberate you, and could not do anything else. If this is not the case it means that something is very wrong.

In the Beginning It's Up to the Teacher

In the beginning it's up to the Teacher to prove him or herself to you *absolutely*. But once they have done so, then it's up to you to prove yourself to the Teacher *absolutely*.

A Secret Relationship

If you are deadly serious and you are lucky enough to find a real Teacher, you will come to a point where the relationship with the Teacher is just like looking into a mirror. You will know that the Teacher knows that you know that the Teacher knows that you know that the Teacher knows that you know...When this is constant there is not much more to say.

The relationship with the Teacher is a secret relationship. It is a secret only between you and the Teacher. Only you and the Teacher know about it. You can try and talk about it with others but you won't be able to touch it. It's a secret based on a mutual recognition that can't be expressed in words.

Go beyond Tragedy and Misery

Go beyond Tragedy and Misery

Face the Truth

Don't Insist

There Is No Block

Finishing Means Ending, Working Out
Means Continuing

See the Way Things Are

Throw It All Away

Go beyond Tragedy and Misery

Q: All I see around me is tragedy and misery.

A: Tragedy and misery are a part of life. If you focus only on tragedy and misery then tragedy and misery will be all that you see. Go beyond tragedy and misery to a place where nothing ever happens. Find that place where no event ever occurred. If you are compulsively fascinated with memory then memories are all that you will see. Compulsive fascination with memory is akin to living in a house with dead, rotting corpses. It is a morbid experience. If you are looking only at dead bodies then the possibility of knowing something fresh and new will be impossible. The happiness I talk about is knowing that which is new in every moment.

There is a brightness and a shine that is ever new. That is the presence of God. That is your own Self.

Face the Truth

Most people do not have the humility that is necessary for Enlightenment. Unable to discriminate clearly, most people react mechanically to whatever passes through their mind's eye. They are endlessly shocked by the contents of their own mind, always surprised at the garbage that arises out of the void. This inability to discriminate with clarity often leads to actions that eventually cause suffering to self and other. People like this are still in kindergarten. There is absolutely nothing to be shocked about. People stick their heads into the garbage can of their worst fears and most dubious desires and seem utterly surprised and perplexed at how they feel helpless and confused after the expedition has been completed. "How did this happen?" they ask themselves.

You need to be serious. If you are able to be serious you will be quiet and still and you will see the way things really are. You will realize that nothing you think makes any difference. You will see how nothing you ever thought makes any difference, and you will see how nothing you ever could think could ever make any difference. Let this in. If you let this in, you will be able to see clearly. You will be able to discriminate. You will be able to extricate yourself from the endless confusion and chaos of thought and memory, fear and desire.

Face the complete illusory nature of your existence. Face it stoically, silently, without moving a muscle. Face it and see the truth. Not many people have the courage to face their own non-existence. If a person does not want to face their own non-existence then they will never, ever be truly Free.

Don't Insist

Q: Is it really possible to escape samsara and attain the realization of Enlightenment right now? I always thought that it would take a long time.

A: Yes, it is possible, but you must stop insisting otherwise. Anybody who says that Enlightenment takes time is actually only insisting on listening to the ego screaming, "No, but I!" "No, but me!" "No, but mine!" None of that has anything to do with Enlightenment. By continually insisting that Enlightenment takes time, you are the expression of samsara itself.

There Is No Block

Q: I feel blocked.

A: You need to devote time to paying attention. When you look at it very closely, the whole idea of being blocked is completely illusory. There is no block. There is only fear and craving.

Q: Are you saying to observe more closely?

A: If you observe more closely you will see that there isn't any block. You will see that there never has been any block. There is no block! Fear and craving create the illusion of a block. There is only fear and craving. There is no block! Do you understand?

Q: What if fear arises in the mind?

A: If there is fear, there is fear. If there is craving, there is craving. The block is only the idea "there is a block." *That* is the problem, that idea only. It is very simple. People find it very hard to understand, but that is all there is to it.

Finishing Means Ending, Working Out Means Continuing

Q: I want to be completely Free, and so I am very interested in understanding where a lot of my past traumas originally began. I feel that maybe this way I will be able to finish with them forever. Am I going in the right direction?

A: If you truly want to be Free, then that means that you are interested only in finishing with *all* of your past right *now*. Finishing with it means leaving it alone. Finishing with it means leaving all of it completely alone, and only then can you be finished with it. Do you understand? Finishing with it means leaving it alone and not picking it up again. Finishing with it *does not mean working it out*. It means leaving it *forever*. True spiritual work only means finishing with and never working out.

This difference between working it out and finishing with it is not known by most seekers. Finishing means ending. Working out means continuing. Most seekers don't understand this difference.

See the Way Things Are

Q: How do I extricate myself from samsara?

A: By seeing the way things are. Be more interested in what you are seeing than in the fact that you may at times feel uncomfortable. You should be more interested in seeing what the whole picture is. Don't focus only on your discomfort. Only then will your understanding deepen. This is what renunciation is all about—being more interested in seeing the way things are than in having things the way you want them to be.

Q: There seems to be a general sense of discomfort in just living, a feeling of "there's something wrong."

A: If you identify with the pain then you will be lost forever. If you identify with the pain as being who you are then there can be no Liberation. That's what creates ego—the idea that there is a problem. That idea makes you feel special and feeling special makes you feel separate. Give up that idea and then you are Free. Give up the infatuation with your problem. That is what everybody has to do.

If you want to know the way things are you only have to open your eyes. You don't have to do anything else. Then throughout the period of a day you will learn everything you need to know about the way things are. All you have to do is pay attention.

Throw It All Away

There is no end to the past. There is no end to it. The more you look into the past the more you will find. It is endless. See how the past has no end. Keep looking and looking and you can spend your whole life looking into the garbage can of the past. The past is like a garbage can that has no bottom to it. Keep pulling out one piece of garbage after another and you will find that the garbage can always remains full. Understand that there is no end to it. See that the past is all dirty garbage. Have the courage to put the cover on top of the garbage can and then throw the whole thing away and wash your hands.

Stop needing to insist that you have a past that is tormenting you. People identify with old feelings of being hurt because it makes them feel special. That's why they are so fascinated by them. Have the courage to throw it all away. The specialness and the morbid comfort that comes from the past is profound ignorance. Want none of it. Identify with none of it. Renounce all the morbid gratification and satisfaction that you derive from dwelling on the pain and agony of your past. It doesn't have to mean anything at all.

Have the courage to renounce the past completely.
Do not allow yourself to be intimidated by the ghosts
and demons that come to tempt you. Renounce them all.
Renounce them all.

Effort

Does Effort Have Any Relationship to Freedom?

Is It Possible for Someone to Realize
Enlightenment without Making Effort?

Does Effort Have Any Relationship to Freedom?

Q: Does effort have any relationship to Freedom?

A: What is important is that you do the right thing, and if you have to make effort, it doesn't make any difference as long as you do the right thing. Some people have to make a lot of effort, and some have to make almost no effort at all—it all depends on the nature of the individual. If one gets attached to the idea of no-effort, that idea can become very fixed and no doubt, an obstacle. On the other hand, if one gets attached to the idea of having to make effort, then that idea can also become an obstacle. Neither of those are what I'm pointing to. Sometimes you have to put your foot on the gas, sometimes you have to put your foot on the brake, sometimes you don't have to do either. What I'm saying is, which direction is the car pointed in at any moment? Everybody's different. From one moment to another, different things are required.

In the end there's absolutely nothing to do, nothing to change and no one to become. When you are no longer interested in the past and you are no longer interested in the future, when you know you're completely helpless, these ideas of effortlessness versus effort won't have any meaning.

Is It Possible for Someone to Realize Enlightenment without Making Effort?

Q: Is it possible for someone to realize Enlightenment without making effort?

A: As long as there is effort to be made then the ego can still have power. But when there is no effort to be made then the ego has no power any longer. That's the whole point.

Letting Go

A State of Constant Amazement

Just Stop

Just Lean Back

What Does It Really Mean to Let Go?

Seeing Things as They Are *Is* Letting Go

Let It End

A State of Constant Amazement

Q: I work at getting out of the way and letting go, but in spite of that I often don't know what the right choices to make are.

A: When you truly get out of the way you will find that you will do the right thing at precisely the right moment. Because of this you will be in a state of constant amazement. Your whole life can be a life of constant amazement but only when you are no longer working at it.

Just Stop

A: Realize that you have been practicing ignorance, unknowingly and unwittingly. Realize that you have been confining and limiting yourself. Realize that this is only a habit that you learned a long time ago.

Q: How can I break that habit?

A: By doing the opposite. By not mechanically limiting your attention to this or that. It is effortless, easy and natural. Just simply stop. Stop trying. Stop trying to overcome, stop trying to avoid, stop trying to arrive. Just stop. Unconditionally stop. Practice absolute renunciation. Do you understand?

Q: Yes.

A: Have you begun?

Q: Yes.

A: Does it feel easy and natural?

Q: No, not yet.

A: Then you have not yet begun.

Just Lean Back

All you have to do is shift a little bit back inside yourself. Just shift back and you might find something very nice. You don't even have to close your eyes. All you have to do is lean back and allow yourself to rest. If you lean back you will realize that you were always off-balance leaning forward. All you have to do is lean back. It's very simple. Leaning back doesn't take any effort. Leaning forward takes a lot of effort. When you lean back you will discover effortlessness. That is happiness. It's just a matter of getting a different perspective. It's a very delicate movement. You have to be aware from somewhere else. Find out where. Once you find it you will feel, "Ah, that's it!" It's like getting a thread through a needle. This has nothing to do with making effort. It has to do with allowing yourself to give up all the effort of becoming. This is only a simple shift of attention from the unreal to the real, and that's all. When you stop making effort, then you will be there. It doesn't take time. Simply seek the insecurity of not-knowing and abide there.

What Does It Really Mean to Let Go?

Q: What does it really mean to let go? Should I just give up what gets in the way?

A: Yes, give up what gets in the way, but that's not enough. For many people who have practiced spiritual disciplines for a long time the idea of giving up what gets in the way is nothing new. Many of these people, in spite of all the effort they have made to give up what gets in their way, usually remain thoroughly in control and still firmly in the grip of their ego. This is because it is their ego that is trying to do the giving up, and it can't work that way. Real giving up has to take place in such a way that the ego in its entirety is given up, *all at once*. This is what letting go really means.

Q: How does this happen?

A: This happens with the dawning of Enlightenment within you. When you begin to recognize a perfect purity that is stronger than the power of your own mind, you will see yourself come to your knees. That *is* the letting go. It is the recognition of that purity alone that consumes the very desire to hold on.

Seeing Things as They Are *Is* Letting Go

Letting go is not something you can do. If you want to let go you only have to see everything as it is. You only need to see everything as it is until you no longer have any doubt about what it is you are looking at. That is all you have to do.

Seeing things as they are *is* letting go. You have to look and look and look again until there is absolutely no mystery about the contents of your own mind. As long as there is any trace of suspicion or doubt about the ultimate nature of any thought, it will be impossible to let go of anything.

Let It End

Q: I'm not interested in seeking anymore. I feel in my heart a very strong urge to have it end.

A: Then let it end, that's all. It's very easy. You just have to open your eyes. When you're ready just open your eyes, it's all very obvious. It's a mystery the way everybody imagines that they don't know. If you are able to reject unconditionally every idea your mind produces, you will be able to accept everything as it is right now. It will all be finished. You will be ecstatic. You will see how nothing has limited your view except a desire to grasp and to know. When you give up the need to grasp and to know you will realize how the very desire to grasp Liberation was blinding you.

If you want it to end you must be able to accept yourself absolutely, as you are now, until you are no longer an issue. You must no longer be interested or fascinated with you. As long as you allow yourself to remain important, then you will only be aware of how you feel — whether you feel happy or unhappy, disturbed or peaceful. When you are no longer interested in you, the splendor that you seek will be all around you.

Allow yourself to realize that you have always been

blessed. Allow yourself to let everything be. Only then will it be possible to realize that blessedness which is always there. If you are so lucky that you are able to let things be, then you have to be prepared for the shock. This blessedness is so awesome that it can shock your whole system. You may feel that you can't contain it. This is what revelation is.

Renounce Time

Renounce Time

If You Hide Behind Time

Renounce Time

Q: How can I wake up?

A: By piercing the veil of illusion.

Q: How do I do that?

A: By giving up all your desires and fears.

Q: How do I do that?

A: By allowing everything to be as it is.

Q: I need to understand that on a deeper level than the intellectual.

A: Then by all means allow that to happen right now. Allow everything to be as it is. Abandon the process of overcoming the past and preparing for the future. All that's involved is the profound renunciation of time itself. It's very simple. But unless this renunciation is complete, it won't work. It has to be unconditional.

Then you will discover true meditation, and that's when the spiritual life begins.

If You Hide Behind Time

If you have a problem with time it means that you have not taken out the time to look deeply into life. You have kept yourself busy and occupied. When you cease to be preoccupied with time a vista can suddenly open up where there is absolutely no limitation. That's when many will shout, "Oh no, no! It's too much! I want to get back to work, I want to get back to my routine." These people are terrified of timelessness!

There is a mystery that is ever-present but is hidden by time. If you hide behind time you won't be able to find this mystery. But if you cease to hide behind time this mystery will become self-evident. The discovery of this mystery will free you from your fear of time and will release you from the sense of being imprisoned by life.

Abandon the Future

Life without a Future

Abandon the Future

Unless...

Life without a Future

It is interesting to explore what it means to have no future. One description of Enlightenment is life without a future. When there is deep contentment and profound understanding the simple fact of being alive can be an extremely thrilling experience. Just walking down the road or having a cup of tea with a friend can be thrilling. Only when you have no doubt that it's all here right now will you recognize that you're on the edge of something very big that has no limit.

When you liberate yourself from the future you will always be on the edge of something very big that has no limit.

Abandon the Future

Q: If I want to be Free what do I need to give up first: the past or the future?

A: Anybody who sincerely wants to be Free should abandon the future. If they do so absolutely, their history will automatically disappear.

Unless...

Unless one has truly abandoned the future, unless one has finished seeking absolutely, and unless the issue of being Free has been solved forever — it will be impossible to see clearly for more than a brief instant.

Meeting the Teacher

When You Meet Your Teacher Seeking
Comes to an End

Meeting the Teacher

A Spontaneous Event

If Liberation Wasn't Given, Then Move On

When You Meet Your Teacher
Seeking Comes to an End

When you finally meet your Teacher all your seeking will come to an end. You will know it. All the endless, esoteric confusion finally will come to an end. When you find your Teacher all will be solved in an instant.

When all your seeking finally comes to an end it won't necessarily mean that you will be a perfectly Enlightened Buddha. But it will mean that something fundamental has surely occurred. You will know, "I have found it, whatever it is I don't know, but I know that I have found it and it has found me."

Meeting the Teacher

Q: Does the ego die only when it is in relationship to the Teacher?

A: The ego doesn't go anywhere, but it can be tricked. People are so identified with thoughts and ideas that they are not aware of who they are. When you meet the Teacher a trick happens. In spite of thoughts, ideas, feelings, and memories, the Self is realized. Yes, in spite of that, the Self is realized. The ego doesn't go anywhere. The ego doesn't change. In spite of that, something happens. Nothing is born. Nothing dies. Something is Realized. This is the trick. This is meeting the Teacher.

A Spontaneous Event

If you are lucky enough to find your Teacher, in that meeting, you will actually begin to see before your very own eyes yourself becoming aligned to your True Self. You will actually feel it happening. This is a spontaneous event in which you begin to feel closer to who you always have been. You will feel more like who you are. You will feel a freedom from identifying yourself with other people and outside events. You will realize a natural condition of being. In this experience there is a profound resonance in a great harmony. There is ecstasy in this release. When you truly meet your Teacher, this is what happens.

If Liberation Wasn't Given, Then Move On

It doesn't matter how much time you have spent with a Teacher—if Liberation wasn't given, then move on. Don't be attached to no-Enlightenment. But if Liberation has been given to you then stop, stop dead in your tracks. The Teacher should give you that experience very quickly. Then it's up to you to live up to it. A real Teacher should demonstrate who they are by giving you that experience of Enlightenment. It's up to you to hold onto it and live up to it. It's up to you to prove yourself worthy of the experience. The big event of Enlightenment should be the beginning of your relationship with a real Teacher. It is on that alone that the bond with the Teacher should be based.

The Teacher and Independence

If You Are Not Interested in Finding Your Own
Perfect Death Then There Is No Point in Seeking
the Guidance of an Enlightened Teacher

You Can't Protect Your Independence and
Realize Freedom at the Same Time

When You Are at One with an Enlightened
Teacher Then Time and Space Cannot Come
between You

If You Are Not Interested in Finding Your Own Perfect Death Then There Is No Point in Seeking the Guidance of an Enlightened Teacher

A: If you decide to seek out the help of a spiritual teacher your first job is to scrutinize that teacher very closely over a period of time. You must find out if that teacher is Enlightened, and you must find out if the teacher's life is indeed a perfect demonstration of his teaching. If you find there is a gap between the teacher's words and actions you should leave him behind. But if you decide that this person is in fact a true Master and that you want his help then you must decide to trust his intention to set you Free.

Q: I welcome the help of an Enlightened Teacher as an assistance to furthering my wisdom, but the idea of giving away the care of my own soul to somebody else frightens me.

A: A teacher of Enlightenment is only interested in one thing: killing you. If the teacher is a true Master and not a charlatan then you have nothing to fear except your own death. If you are serious it means that you want to go to a place that you do not yet understand. It is a place that you may have read about, heard about and even glimpsed yourself, but as yet it still remains unknown to you. The teacher should be an expert in this unknown terrain. If the teacher is fully Enlightened he will have a perspective that you do not yet have. You cannot perfectly discern the way unless you are fully Realized yourself. Either you know where you are going and how you are going to get there or you do not.

If you are not interested in finding your own perfect death then there is no point in seeking the guidance of an Enlightened Teacher.

You Can't Protect Your Independence and Realize Freedom at the Same Time

Q: I worry about dependency.

A: The path of Truth is not a path of independence. The path of Truth is a path of total, absolute dependence on the Truth. If one meets a real Teacher it's very difficult to have only a casual involvement. Ultimately it ends up being either complete involvement or no involvement at all. This is because the nature of what is being shared is Absolute. That is why it demands everything. What is demanded is your individuality. It is a wrestling match between the Teacher and the student. That is what the spiritual struggle is all about.

Q: There is something about giving up my individuality that is terrifying.

A: It is to receive help in facing that fear that you go to a Teacher. Don't be so concerned about dependence or independence — just be concerned with being Free. You can't protect your independence and realize Freedom at the same time.

When You Are at One with an Enlightened Teacher Then Time and Space Cannot Come between You

Q: When I am in the presence of my Teacher I feel intimately at one with her. When I spend prolonged periods of time away from my Teacher I often start to experience a distance and a separation that is painful and confusing.

A: If you are at one with an Enlightened Teacher then time and space cannot come between you. One with the Teacher means one with yourself. Your true Self cannot be inhibited by time and space.

When you have experienced and understood the teaching of Enlightenment — *you have to live it.* When you begin to live the teachings without conditions then you become the Teacher. What the Teacher teaches and what you do will be one and the same. When you are ready and willing to accept the teaching of Enlightenment without conditions and are ready to give every breath of your life to living that Enlightenment perfectly, then and only then will you and a true Teacher of Enlightenment be one.

Understanding

Seek Understanding

Seek Understanding

To Be Free Means to Understand

Seek Understanding

The most important thing to seek for is understanding—not an explosion. Seek for understanding
and let understanding do its work. Don't look for an
explosion, explosions aren't necessarily going to do it.
An explosion will only be enough in a very ripe and
ready individual. Seek that understanding that makes
perfect sense. On the other side of perfect understanding
is the Beyond.

To Be Free Means to Understand

In the deepest and most profound sense, what it is to be Free means to *understand*. This means knowing before cognition, before thought. The recognition of *that* is what being Free is. Thoughts and feelings come and go, but that knowing doesn't go anywhere. When you understand that knowing to be your own Self, prior to the entire universe, you will no longer care about coming and going. You will no longer draw any conclusions about who you are or who you're not. It is the discovery of this knowing alone that will set you Free. All wisdom flows from that. When everything disappears you will realize that indivisible, unchanging fact out of which everything arises. Knowing that and being rooted in that without effort and without choice *is* Liberation. It is from this knowing that you witness the whole drama of life.

Hold onto Nothing

Realize Perfect Innocence

Hold onto Nothing

Cling Only to Freedom Alone

Realizing Total Insecurity Is What the Goal Is

Realize Perfect Innocence

Realize perfect innocence and abide there always. The realization of perfect innocence is Self-knowledge. Innocence is what we knew ourselves to be before we knew anything else. Before we knew anything at all, we knew this purity. Coming upon the perfect purity of this innocence, we are overwhelmed with awe, wonder, mystery and devotion.

When you are lost in innocence you are not holding onto anything, because there is such total trust that there is absolutely no need to hold onto anything. There is the knowledge that everything is perfect. The awareness has been released because there is no longer any need to hold on. There is no longer fear of loss, no longer fear of losing anything. It is this openness that is the state of Freedom.

Hold onto Nothing

Q: When I experience profound insight it often slips away. It becomes only a memory and I'm always afraid that it won't come back.

A: That is because your insight is not deep enough. You have not yet understood that there is nothing to lose and nothing to gain. Don't hold onto anything. When you are free of having to understand there is only knowing. When you abide in that knowing what you need to understand will come to you. You don't have to walk around grasping onto understanding with your mind — that will only clutter up your brain.

Q: I've been holding onto understanding.

A: Hold onto nothing. Everything has to go. That's what surrender is. I am happy because I know without any doubt that there is nothing to hold onto.

Q: I have to be sure of that.

A: Don't wait to be sure. Don't wait for the next experience. Don't wait for the next confirmation.

Let go now.

Cling Only to Freedom Alone

Q: This morning a state of purity came over me and I felt like a little child. What came to me at that moment was, "To enter the Kingdom of Heaven you must be innocent."

A: That's right. To enter the Kingdom of Heaven you must be innocent. The innocence that you are referring to is humility.

Q: When I was in that state of purity, I saw a flower in a way that I had never seen it before. That moment seemed infinite. I'm trying to cling to the state that I experienced in that moment.

A: Do not cling to states, cling only to Freedom alone. Freedom transcends conditions. Freedom means Free. Free from this or that, including bliss. To be Free means to be Awake. That's what Enlightenment is all about. To be Enlightened means to understand this deeply. Understanding this alone can set you Free. I'm not talking about a state. I'm talking about a realization that is transcendent.

Realizing Total Insecurity
Is What the Goal Is

A: Everyone wants to find something that they can be sure of. But if you look deeply all you can ever find is total insecurity. Realizing total insecurity is what the goal is. When you accept total insecurity all the time, you feel very comfortable all the time.

Q: What do you mean by accepting total insecurity?

A: Facing the Truth. Seeing that the security that the mind always seeks for does not exist. When that is accepted you are at one with Truth and bliss.

Q: Is the Truth insecure also?

A: No, it's very secure, very dependable. Just abandon the illusion of security and all of the endless seeking for it. Just let go of this false idea. Let go of it completely. Don't just think about it and read about it or meditate on the possibility.

Q: Are you talking about reconditioning the mind intellectually?

A: No, I'm talking about deconditioning it, not reconditioning it. If the mind is deconditioned then it's not holding onto anything that's unreal. You will know the Truth in every moment because you won't be struggling to see anything other than it truly is.

Mind

There Is Only One Mind

The Corruption of God

Mind Is Not an Obstacle

The Mind Is a Berry Patch

Question:

There Is Only One Mind

Q: What is the mind?

A: The mind is a mechanical process. If you look closely enough you will see that you could not be that mechanical process because you are observing it. You are watching it move. *You* are not moving. *It* is moving. When you see this you will find out what the problem has been all along. Then you will say, "Oh my God, look what I've been doing! All these years I thought I was my mind, I thought I was my thoughts and feelings, and because I thought I was my thoughts and feelings, I acted like a fool!" It is very humiliating and humbling when you realize that you have been a puppet all your life. You need to look deeply and find this out for yourself. Then you will realize there is only one mind, and you will see how everybody is lost in the same dream.

The Corruption of God

Q: My mind seems to always keep going and this disturbs me very much. It constantly interferes with my meditation.

A: Your mind disturbs you only because you are fascinated by it.

Q: If I relinquish this fascination will I be Free?

A: Yes. The end of that fascination is the birth of Enlightenment.

Q: I feel that I still have to understand more before I can relinquish this fascination.

A: Your need to understand more is the expression of doubt. You are bargaining with God. You will never find Freedom that way. You cannot bargain with Him. To Him you can only offer everything. The degree to which you are ready to give everything for that Freedom is the exact degree to which you will be Free.

Q: I can't give everything because my mind always wants to know more. It wants to be sure that in that absolute giving there will be safety.

A: The mind is only a machine. It has no self-nature. It is not your mind that hesitates. It is *you*. You fear God and because of this, you hesitate. The ego is nothing more than the doubt that your fear of God arises from. What gives the mind the illusion of self-nature is your fascination with doubt and fear.

The ego is the illusion of self-nature that you alone give to the mind. That is the corruption of God.

Mind Is Not an Obstacle

Q: It's difficult to stop the obstacles coming in.

A: There aren't any obstacles.

Q: My mind is an obstacle.

A: No it's not. There are no obstacles. You are speaking about obstacles but there is nothing obstructing you. Realize that! It's much easier to dwell on the idea of there being an obstacle than facing the fact that there are no obstacles. Yes, that's much more difficult.

The Mind Is a Berry Patch

Imagine that the mind is a berry patch and that individual thoughts are like the berries in the patch. Imagine you are standing in front of the berry patch. As you stand in front of the berry patch you notice the different kinds of berries in the patch. You easily notice that some of the berries are sweet, that some are sour and that some are completely rotten. The sweet ones you eat freely and the sour and rotten ones you don't touch. And when your stomach is full you don't even touch the sweet ones.

The existence of the berry patch in no way disturbs or inhibits the perfect integrity of the universe. The existence of the berry patch in no way demonstrates the existence of any problem or conflict. A problem only arises when due to our own blind ignorance we stuff every berry that our eye comes into contact with in our mouth; rotten, sweet or sour. Then we wonder why our stomachs are upset all the time!

Stop the habit of compulsively eating every berry that comes into your sight. Take the time and make the effort to see whether the berry you happen to be staring at is sweet, rotten or sour. Never under any circumstance allow yourself to eat a sour or rotten berry. Eat only the sweet ones, and have the sense to eat them only when you are hungry.

Question:

What was your relationship to thought before you were convinced that there was a problem?

No Identity

Realize Objectivity

When You Have No Face

What Does It Feel Like to Be Nowhere?

Afraid of Losing Everything

If You Have No Ideas about Who You Are

Realize Objectivity

Self-image is always a dark corner. Most people are suffering from the same agony, tormented by ideas of who they are, who they want to be and who they don't want to be. It helps when you realize that this predicament *is* the human condition. It helps when you realize that almost everybody is suffering in this same misery. Realizing this can help. It can help you to see through the illusion that you are suffering in your misery isolated and alone. Because of this idea many people feel sorry for themselves. When you realize that this is the average condition of almost everyone it is the beginning of a big change in perspective.

Realize it's not "your" problem. Realize that it is *the* problem. Realize that this one mistake is the crux of the human predicament. Try and make the effort to depersonalize every aspect of your experience, from the gross to the subtle.

Realize objectivity. It's the only way out.

When You Have No Face

Our hearts are imprisoned by our mind and intellect, locked inside by a prison of ideas about reality which creates a very convincing illusion. Become aware of the overwhelming influence of memory on your experience. Realize how pervasive the influence of memory is. See how memory, and desires that arise from memory, corrupt your awareness. Pay close attention and see the effect. It is important to be aware of the incredible subtlety in all of this.

When you have no memory you have no face. When you have no face you are happy, and you are at rest. When you have no face there is no longer anything to work out, no longer anything to overcome and no longer anything to understand.

What Does It Feel Like to Be Nowhere?

Q: If I get Enlightened where would I stand in relationship to my personal history and identity?

A: Nowhere.

Q: What does it feel like to be nowhere?

A: It feels free. Independent. It feels like a mask has been taken off. You cannot imagine who you are anymore. When people call your name you no longer have any idea who they know you to be. You honestly won't know. Even if you try and make an effort to conjure up what you appear like in the eyes of others, you won't be able to. Most people have a very fixed, sure idea of who they are, who they have been, and who they want to become. When you wake up you might still have some vague memory of who you thought you were before you realized that you had no idea—but that will be all there is left.

Afraid of Losing Everything

Q: How can I come to terms with the fear I feel when I contemplate the possibility of being truly Free?

A: You have to be clearly aware of what it is that you are afraid of. You are afraid that you are going to lose the identification with the thoughts that you recognize as being you. There is fear that the recognition will be lost and that you won't know who you are anymore. Even if you know that when you let go you will be Free, the fear is so great that you hold on anyway. It is only the fear of being without the security of knowing who you are.

Q: That's what frightens me.

A: That means it was the right answer.

Q: Could you say it again?

A: You are afraid of losing everything that you have based your entire life on. You are afraid all will be lost and that you will be in an unknown place, completely alone.

If you look closely you will see who you think you are is only thoughts tied together. In your mind's eye that is who you think you are. If you have no thoughts and no memory there is nobody left. You are afraid of being without a personality that you can recognize as being you. That is why you are terrified.

If You Have No Ideas about Who You Are

Q: You have said that ideas can be a prison.

A: Yes. Especially ideas about ourselves and ideas about God.

Q: My ideas about God are the most difficult to let go of.

A: When you have no ideas about who you are then you will know God automatically.

Love

Where Is Love in the Search for and
Discovery of Enlightenment?

The Power of Love

The Discovery of Impersonal Love
Is the Only Way Out

What Is Loving?

Where Is Love in the Search for and Discovery of Enlightenment?

Q: Where is Love in the search for and discovery of Enlightenment?

A: At the beginning, at the middle, and at the end.

Q: Can you say more than that?

A: How is it possible to say more than that? Love is the source, Love is the vehicle. Love is the prime mover and the prime doer. Love is the source of Enlightenment. The expression of Enlightenment is Love.

The source of Love and the source of Enlightenment are one and the same.

The Power of Love

Q: What is the power of Love?

A: The power of Love is what forces a human being to take life seriously.

Q: I feel like it's something I want to understand.

A: You can't understand Love. Love is not of the mind. You have to experience Love yourself and then you will understand. When you start to see everything fall away, then you will know what Love is.

The Discovery of Impersonal Love
Is the Only Way Out

Q: Is True Love an impersonal love?

A: Yes. You will have found that True Love when you are no longer distinguishing between the personal and the impersonal. You will have found True Love only when they have become one and the same.

Q: Is it a challenge to love in this way?

A: Impersonally? Oh yes! The discovery of impersonal love is the only way out. It is only loving impersonally that will allow you to let go to the degree necessary to realize that perfect objectivity that enables a human being to see clearly. It is impersonal love alone that reveals the perspective that is needed to see things as they are.

What Is Loving?

Q: Can you talk more about love? What is loving?

A: Loving is Being.

Q: What does it mean to be egoless?

A: Egoless means you know what the ego is and you know what it is not. When you know what the ego is and you know what it is not, then you discover this beautiful, sweet, simple Truth — that your true nature is Love. When you cease to be infatuated with yourself as being a separate entity, compulsively preoccupied with problems and ambitions, then you will realize lovingness. When you are unpreoccupied, this is the natural state. "Oh my God, what a discovery!" you will say.

Ego preoccupation is the sole obstruction to the realization of lovingness. What does it mean to be egoless? The realization of lovingness. That's what it means.

The True Heart

Imagine a Throne

The Discovery of the True Heart
Is the Discovery of Intuition

Finding the Heart Is a Very Big Event

The True Heart

A Perfect Condition

Imagine a Throne

Imagine a throne, and imagine that your mind is seated on that throne. This is the position and condition in which most people live their lives, prostrated before and in submission to the mind. This position and condition is called ignorance, is called delusion and is called samsara. When for some mysterious reason the mind and the heart trade places you will suddenly realize a completely new and radically different perspective. With the heart now seated on the throne and the mind now in prostration before and in submission to the heart everything will look very different. One will find a new perspective impossible to imagine. This altered position and new condition is Enlightenment. This altered position and new condition is the goal of all spiritual seeking and is the fulfillment of the heart's true longing for emancipation.

The Discovery of the True Heart
Is the Discovery of Intuition

The discovery of the True Heart is the discovery of intuition. In that discovery is the beginning of the end of ignorance. That is because in the discovery of intuition you begin to recognize that you already know the answer. You see that you do have the ability to judge, to discern, and to know what is true. In the discovery of the True Heart, you begin to eliminate all authorities, and find true wisdom.

It is then that the whole cycle of doubt can finally come to an end.

Finding the Heart Is a Very Big Event

Many people say, "Just follow your heart." Most people have not found their heart. How can you follow your heart if you haven't found it first? You have to find your heart first; only then can you follow it.

Truly finding the heart is a very big event. Few people actually do.

The True Heart

Q: What is the True Heart?

A: The True Heart is the place where you always know how things are. It is a place of absolute confirmation and absolute affirmation. It is where everything is always revealed. If someone is truly Enlightened then the Heart I am speaking about is their only home. It is the source of who and what they are. In this True Heart everything is always known. It is always perfect fullness. Out of that perfect fullness comes self-arising wisdom.

When you discover the True Heart you will know how to walk through life with courage and dignity. When you discover the True Heart you will know what you are doing here.

A Perfect Condition

The goal of all seeking is the discovery and realization of a perfect condition in which there is no longer any need to distinguish between the heart and the mind.

Detachment

In Detachment Is Where the Enlightened
Mind Flourishes

It Is Detachment That Allows Us to Realize
What Love Is

Detachment Is a Free Gift of Awareness Itself

Remain Detached Even from Bliss

In Detachment Is Where the Enlightened Mind Flourishes

There is a great mystery in profound surrender. In profound surrender there is detachment. Being profoundly detached means being completely involved and completely uninvolved simultaneously. Perfect Enlightenment is possible when there is no gap between involvement and uninvolvement.

In detachment is where the Enlightened mind flourishes.

It Is Detachment That Allows Us to Realize What Love Is

It is detachment that allows us to realize what love is. I'm not speaking about the kind of love you feel for your children or the kind of love you feel for a lover—I'm speaking about a love that is unbearable. The kind of love I'm speaking about will bring you to your knees. This love and detachment are synonymous. If you are unwilling to let go then this kind of love you cannot know. To be worthy of this kind of love you have to give up all your ideas and all your attachments.

Love and death go together. If you want to know what love is you have to pay a big price for it. You have to die to the known. You have to die to your lover. You have to die to your children. You have to die to your friends. You have to die to the whole universe. Then you will find out what love is. Only then you will understand what detachment is all about.

Detachment Is a Free Gift of Awareness Itself

Q: I realize that I can be detached from my mind.

A: Are you sure? Are you sure you can be detached from your mind?

Q: My experience of the mind is that I watch thoughts and feelings pass or I can choose to be with them.

A: There's more to it, there is something way beyond all that. It gets interesting only when you realize that you never had anything to do with the mind. It gets interesting when you find out that it was *never* you. When you realize this so completely that it ceases to touch you, then you no longer have to make any effort to censor or control in any way. You won't have to make any effort to pay attention because you will be attentive naturally. This is when detachment is spontaneously realized. It is an ongoing experience that reveals itself to the observer, by itself. The experience of detachment and the awareness of detachment is a fact of life, a free gift of awareness itself! Also there is bubbling joy, because detachment itself *is* joy — they are the *same thing*. What does this mean? "I'm Free! I'm Free! I'm Free!"

Remain Detached Even from Bliss

Q: Is bliss a by-product of knowing or is it just a feeling?

A: Bliss is knowing and feeling. They are not separate. All knowledge is in bliss. Most people, because they are ignorant, only are aware of how they feel. If they experience bliss they are only aware of feeling good. They are not evolved enough to see all knowledge and the whole universe in that bliss. Most people can't see it. If you look beyond feelings, everything is there for you. That's why it's imperative to remain detached, even from bliss. In that detachment, you will find wisdom.

Awareness

The Awareness Is Always There

What Does It Mean to Be Awake?

Quality of Attention

Self-Realization Is the Discovery of Pure
Consciousness

The Awareness Is Always There

Q: I have heard it said many times, "You must be aware all the time." Does this awareness arise of itself?

A: The awareness is always there. But because we are compulsively focused on and paying attention only to the past and future, we miss it. When our attention rises up or goes back, we suddenly recognize that we have been aware all the time. Because we were paying attention only to little specks of dirt on the floor we didn't bother to look up and see everything else. It sounds simple, but it's a very complex process that we are constantly involved in. Unless on a very deep level we let go of all of it, it will be impossible to recognize that we are aware — even though we always are.

What Does It Mean to Be Awake?

Q: I want to be more awake in my daily life. I find as I go through the day that I'm being inattentive and too lax about really being awake.

A: Some people, when suddenly they find themselves in the bathroom brushing their teeth not being able to remember how they got there, feel this means that they are not awake. To truly be awake has nothing to do with that. To truly be awake means always being true to the desire to be Free. Moment-to-moment attention means not losing touch with that. Being awake means being absolutely true to that desire alone. Lapses of attention when the mind wanders here or there do not necessarily indicate anything about being asleep or awake. To wake up means to find one's own heart. Staying awake means never doing anything that would jeopardize or compromise that purity in any way.

Quality of Attention

Q: I'm concerned about the quality of my attention.

A: The quality of your attention depends only on where your heart truly is. The quality of your attention depends on the kind of person that you are. The kind of person that you are is reflected by what it is that you want. The quality of your attention depends only on how selfish or not selfish you really are. The quality of your attention depends only on that.

Self-Realization Is the Discovery of Pure Consciousness

The realization of Enlightenment is the recognition of *consciousness itself*. Most people are not aware of consciousness. They are only aware of the objects that manifest in consciousness.

Self-realization is the discovery of pure consciousness.

What makes you happy is the knowledge of consciousness itself. When you realize that, you are happy. It is when consciousness itself is *very* self-evident that you will be most happy. In the midst of this awareness, there is the apparent existence of this world. It is not your recognition of the presence of the world that makes you happy. It is the awareness of consciousness itself that is the source of your true happiness. When the world disappears, there will only be *that*.

There Is No Other

Pierce the Illusion of Separation

There Is No Other

What Does It Mean to No Longer Exist?

Penetrating Clarity Destroys All Illusions

You Have to Be Willing to Leave Everyone
Else Behind

Pierce the Illusion of Separation

Q: How can I bridge the gap between the separation that I feel and the longing in my heart?

A: Pierce the illusion of separation. Realize and know the timeless. Know the presence of the uncreated. Then this whole question of how to connect one thing with another won't arise in your mind. There will be nothing to connect, because there won't be any separation. Separation is only an idea, pure imagination. To discover what I'm talking about you have to let go of all of your assumptions—and look again.

If you are holding up the mirror of the past all the time, you can't see beyond it to infinity.

There Is No Other

Q: Since I've met you I'm experiencing a tremendous upheaval.

A: Isn't it a glorious upheaval?

Q: It feels heartbreaking.

A: Why?

Q: It's the feeling of my heart opening.

A: Do you feel passionate love?

Q: I feel a passionate hurt, a passionate ache. I feel an aloneness that seems very profound. It goes beyond childhood, beyond mother or father...

A: The profound aloneness that you are feeling is none other than the echo of the Absolute. The absolute truth is — *there is no other*. Do you understand? *There is no other!* With this realization one can experience a profound aloneness. This profound aloneness is simply the truth of there being no other. Do you understand?

Q: Yes. Thank you.

What Does It Mean to No Longer Exist?

Q: Enlightened people often say they have died and no longer exist. What does this mean?

A: They are referring to the realization that one doesn't exist as separate from everyone and everything. When one truly realizes this and recognizes this deeply, the effect is that self-importance dissolves. This means that the need to be inferior or superior, to overcome or become has been destroyed, burned out and finished with forever. This happens when the habitual and compulsive fascination with the personal has finally come to an end, and what's left is a liberated human being who says they have died and no longer exist. What does this mean? The struggle is over.

Penetrating Clarity Destroys All Illusions

True loneliness will be discovered by any human being bold enough to see things as they are. If you would be so brave and are so fortunate to realize that which is true, then it is unavoidable at the same time that you will also see that which is untrue. The more you become aware of that which is real, then much of what you thought was real will suddenly be seen as unreal. For many this can be quite hard to bear.

Penetrating clarity destroys all illusions. When you are no longer interested in illusions, then you will find yourself alone. When illusion is seen through, you will discover true loneliness. You will only be with yourself then.

You Have to Be Willing to Leave Everyone Else Behind

If you want to be Free then you have to be willing to leave everyone else behind. You have to be willing to say goodbye forever. You have to be willing to give up the pretense that there was ever another.

If you want to discover the One, you have to abandon the many. You cannot have both.

You Are in the World
No Matter Where You Are

You Are in the World No Matter Where You Are

Doing Is Being as Much as Not-Doing Is Being

Truth Is Not an Object

You Are in the World
No Matter Where You Are

Q: Is it possible to pursue Enlightenment wholeheartedly while still living in the world?

A: The world is not the problem. In a Himalayan cave you may find the same chaos that exists in the world. All chaos in the world originates in the mind.

You are in the world no matter where you are.

Doing Is Being as Much as Not-Doing Is Being

Q: I'm wondering why I get so caught up in doing instead of just being.

A: The only way you can be caught up in doing rather than Being is when you have misconstrued ideas about what doing means and about what Being means. Being does not in any way imply not-doing. Doing is Being as much as not-doing is Being. All is Being, including all motion and all stillness.

Q: I feel tension when I have to do something.

A: Tension is part of Being also.

Truth Is Not an Object

Q: How can I apply the idea of non-attachment to my daily life?

A: Truth is not an object. It can only be Realized. You cannot do anything with it. When you realize this questions like these will seem utterly absurd to you.

Fear of Freedom

The Questionless State

On the Other Side of Freedom Terror Always
Lays in Wait

Limitlessness Strikes Fear in the Hearts of Men

Serious Seekers Cannot Run

Is There Room for Fear in the Spiritual Life?

The Questionless State

When all your questions have been answered you can enjoy the questionless state. For most people this is a terrifying state to be in: suspended between question and answer. Between question and answer there is a vacuum. For the mind this vacuum is a terrifying place — because the mind recognizes that in that vacuum, it does not exist.

On the Other Side of Freedom
Terror Always Lays in Wait

On the other side of Freedom terror always lays in wait. Anybody who is seeking for and interested in finding true Freedom may be plagued by fear. Because if you say, "I seek Freedom," it means that you are seeking that which has no limit. Terror may come when looking into the limitlessness of that which has no beginning and no end. To the finite ego that which is infinite has to be terrifying.

When you dare to break down all barriers fear will rush in and try to prevent you from succeeding. When all ideas are being shaken there's a chance you may step beyond them, and the ego has no existence where there is no idea of limitation.

Glimpsing this possibility is for many quite terrifying.

Limitlessness Strikes Fear in the Hearts of Men

Q: I feel like everything in my life is shattering. I feel my ego screaming.

A: That's the whole idea.

Q: Should I just stay with it?

A: The realization of the Absolute is perception and awareness of that which has no limits or boundaries. Awareness of limitlessness strikes fear in the hearts of men, because no limits means the realization of the ego's non-existence. You do not need to do anything about this. When you feel this fear in a particularly striking manner know that this is the Absolute, but seen from the point of view of the ego. The ego means an idea of limitation that is compulsively imposed upon that which has no limit, and as long as there is a compulsive imposition of limitation on that which is unlimited then fear is going to be the result.

Serious Seekers Cannot Run

When faced with the possibility of real Freedom, many who think they want to be Free turn tail and run. When terror starts to reveal itself they run back to their holes. The strength of mind necessary to stay firmly in the pure intention to be Free is in the weak-minded lost quickly due to cowardice. Fear can dissolve all clarity, objectivity and any possibility of knowing that perspective which is absolutely true. The weak-minded are unable to recognize that in the face of Freedom fear is always and only temptation to doubt. Doubt is Maya's face revealing itself. It will always try and tempt the weak-minded to turn tail and run. Usually it succeeds. Very few have the clarity and purity of intention that is necessary to face the wall of fear that rises up. In the face of fear the weak-minded never doubt or question the fear itself. They are easily swayed by crude thoughts and strong feelings. They run terrified from the gates of Nirvana back into the hell of the limitation of their own mind. The weak-minded easily betray the heart because they lack the courage necessary to face the unknown. Without that courage they will lack the all-important discrimination necessary to discern the real from the unreal.

Serious seekers for Freedom cannot run. They know they no longer have any choice. They know they will face what must be faced, because they know they must succeed. These lucky few discover something very unexpected: Liberation in this birth.

Is There Room for Fear in the Spiritual Life?

Q: Is there room for fear in the spiritual life?

A: Yes there's room for fear in the spiritual life. There is infinite room for fear in the spiritual life. But there is one thing you must keep in mind: in the spiritual life there is no room for hesitation.

Surrender Is Liberation

Surrender Is Liberation

Realize You Were Never Attached

How Do You Balance Surrender and
Independence?

Surrender Means No Strategies Whatsoever

The Two Aspects of Surrender

Surrender Is Choicelessness

Surrender Is Liberation

The path of Enlightenment is not for everybody, because true Enlightenment demands total surrender. For many the idea of surrender is distasteful. They fear that surrender means being a slave, without realizing that it was because they felt enslaved in the first place that they sought Liberation. The mind finds the concept of surrender unacceptable because it is so absolute, so black and white and so uncompromising. Surrender only means ceasing to submit to that which is non-Self or other than Self. Surrender only means ceasing to submit to that which is unreal, untrue, false and illusory. Sooner or later it will become obvious that there is simply no choice and no other way for anyone who wants to be Free. In the end all spiritual practice points finally to surrender alone.

Realize You Were Never Attached

Q: I have always understood surrender to mean letting go of attachment in every moment. Is that correct?

A: No. Surrender comes from the realization that you were never attached in the first place. When you realize that fact, the conditioned grasping which usually motivates most human behavior doesn't make sense anymore. Surrender has nothing to do with reminding yourself every moment to let go. Surrender is the result of realizing that you were never attached to anything at any moment. Realize this very deeply and you will experience the ecstatic freedom that comes from this realization.

How Do You Balance Surrender and Independence?

Q: How do you balance surrender and independence?

A: Surrender and independence do not need to be balanced because ultimately true surrender and real independence are the same thing. You have to experience profound surrender in order to realize the dynamic independence that is the result of such surrender. To win this independence you have to be willing to sacrifice everything you have been clinging to, including every single idea you have about yourself. You may find that to be quite an excruciating experience. But if you can get through it you will discover a new and different personality manifesting that is free from all the fetters of fixed ideas. True independence comes from the confidence in that discovery. In that discovery there is profound self-reliance.

Surrender Means No Strategies Whatsoever

Q: I have experienced what surrender means many times but I continually lose that understanding and find myself in the process of looking for it again and again.

A: The meaning of surrender transcends loss or gain, even of understanding. This is because surrender leads you beyond what you can understand directly to what you can know—but never understand. Beyond understanding means beyond the mind, beyond the ego, beyond any reference. The acknowledgement, realization and acceptance of that which is beyond understanding is surrender. Surrender makes any strategy that the mind can come up with to take you beyond itself null and void. There is no strategy that can reach that which is beyond the mind except to cease with all strategies whatsoever. That is surrender.

That which is always beyond the mind and ego is always the ultimate challenge for the mind and ego. This is why surrender is the ultimate challenge and it's from the perspective of that challenge that the whole drama of existence is profound and fascinating.

The Two Aspects of Surrender

Q: Is surrender a conscious choice?

A: There are two aspects of surrender. One aspect is unconscious and the other is conscious. Both are equally important and rarely understood. Both must occur in a deep and profound way within an individual for a true and full Enlightenment to be able to arise out of what usually turns out to be only an experience.

The unconscious aspect of surrender happens by itself. This event is involuntary, spontaneous and in no way a matter of will. This is because the mind is not involved. The conscious aspect of surrender is the fully conscious recognition that the process or fact of surrender has occurred or is occurring. The conscious choice to submit absolutely to that which has already taken place is the conscious aspect of surrender.

Both aspects of surrender, unconscious and conscious, must occur equally and completely. If both aspects of surrender do not occur equally and completely the result cannot be full Liberation. The result will be a state of surrender that is still conditional. Only unconditional surrender, which is absolute, results in complete and final emancipation.

Surrender Is Choicelessness

Surrender occurs when you come to a point when you no longer have any choice. You cannot understand what surrender is as long as you still are trying to give something up or trying to attain something. When you realize this choicelessness you come upon a condition that is like a free-fall, a place which is located neither here nor there. Beyond all possibilities there is no longer any question of shoulds and shouldn'ts, coulds or couldn'ts. One has realized a place beyond all possibilities. The direct realization of that place, of that perspective, of that absolute choicelessness, is the true realization of surrender. After you have jumped off a cliff and you are in the midst of falling freely, when you have lost sight of the cliff above you and have lost all memory of the ground below you, then you will understand what surrender is. Only after you've already jumped and you're freely falling can you truly understand what surrender means, not one moment before.

Only when you are in the condition of surrender itself can you understand what it actually is. You cannot understand what surrender is if you want something, even if what you want is Liberation. Surrender is its own condition, it's not something you can do.

Renunciation

Renunciation Is Living Death

Renunciation Is Living Death

When You Become a Giver

The Fire of Your Heart Must Burn Brightly

What Is Renunciation?

Renunciation Is Living Death

If you want to be Free, there's only one path home and that is renunciation.

It doesn't matter what teacher you go to, and it doesn't matter what tradition you follow. In the end the only path to Enlightenment is renunciation alone. Some people, because of pride, are unable to renounce the mind. That's why they continue to struggle and that's why they continue to suffer. It's only because they have so much pride that they can't renounce their own minds. The humility necessary for renunciation is not there. Without profound humility there is no possibility of renunciation.

True renunciation is the ultimate risk. It's living your own death.

When You Become a Giver

When you decide to accept the full teaching of Enlightenment as your own life—that's when something very important happens. That's when you stop being a taker. That's when you become a giver. A taker is someone who still wants for themselves. A taker is not yet ready to accept full responsibility for being Free.

The Enlightened life has only to do with giving. The Enlightened life, which is the holy life, is a life of renunciation and that could only mean giving up. *True* renunciation for the holy life means giving up everything for it.

The Fire of Your Heart Must Burn Brightly

Q: How can I be successful in renouncing my ignorance?

A: The fire of your heart must burn brightly. That fire will give you all the energy, strength and presence of mind to bear with, understand and ultimately see through your own mind. That fire will be your meditation and in that fire your ignorance, which is all your wrong ideas, will burn.

What Is Renunciation?

Q: What role does renunciation play in the spiritual life?

A: Renunciation is the very essence of the spiritual life. Giving up everything in the way of perfect Liberation is the first part of renunciation. The second part of renunciation is making sure one does not ever begin to acquire anything that could in any way obscure that perfect Liberation. Realization is one thing, but keeping it is another matter. The spiritual life is a life of renunciation because to constantly achieve perfect success, one must abide in such a condition that absolutely nothing can be accumulated.

Q: What does renunciation look like practically?

A: True renunciation is an inner matter. But outer renunciation often can serve to facilitate a change in perspective from one of constantly wanting to simply being.

Deep Experiences Are Not Enough

Deep Experiences Are Not Enough

How Do I Relate This Experience to My Life?

It Is Not the Experience of Enlightenment
That Matters

Everybody Wants to Get Enlightened
but Nobody Wants to Change

Deep Experiences Are Not Enough

Spiritual experiences should serve as a catalyst for change that affects every aspect of the personality. Unless change occurs spiritual experiences are worthless. Among seekers deep experiences are quite common, but deep experiences are not enough; because people can realize absolutely everything and still not change at all.

When there has been Realization and profound revelation can a person live up to that which has been revealed? Can a person live up to that ecstasy in every aspect of their life? Most cannot.

The gift of Grace is free. But can a person honor it totally and completely? That's very different. That's when a great sacrifice comes in.

How Do I Relate This Experience to My Life?

Q: I recently had an experience where I was overwhelmed by a flash of blazing light. It left me feeling very excited and at the same time deeply at peace. How do I relate this experience to my life?

A: Why do you need to be able to relate that experience to your life? *You should relate your life to that experience!* That experience is potentially much bigger than your life. If you are lucky that experience will destroy your life entirely. If you are lucky your whole life will dissolve into that blazing light. Then you will be truly Free.

Spiritual experiences are for one purpose only. They enable you to realize the impersonal. If you are lucky your experience will be so profound that it will result in your complete destruction. Then you will see things very differently. Then questions like, "Where does this fit in?" will fall away forever.

It Is Not the Experience
of Enlightenment That Matters

It is not the experience of Enlightenment that matters. It is only the ego's relationship to that experience that has any meaning. Two different individuals could undergo the very same spiritual experience and the ego of one will relate to the event in one way and the ego of the other will relate to that event in a very different manner. The very essence of an individual is revealed in the way they relate to experiences of bliss, emptiness, insight and illumination.

Revelatory experiences themselves do not transform anyone. It is only the inherent readiness of an individual to accept what is revealed in these experiences that can truly transform them.

Everybody Wants to Get Enlightened but Nobody Wants to Change

Q: I have had fantastic spiritual episodes where I was convinced that I was Enlightened but soon discovered that I was far from it. This has happened several times. What went wrong?

A: The problem is that something hasn't happened. A leap has not yet been taken. A lot has been revealed, but the leap has not occurred. Fundamentally, identification is still with the mind. In spite of the fact that you have seen beyond your mind, there is still primarily identification with the mind. What hasn't happened is a shift to identification with that which has nothing to do with the mind. To be truly successful, this shift cannot be only a temporary interlude. It must be permanent and irreversible. You may have fantastic experiences, but they are usually not enough.

Everybody wants to get Enlightened, but nobody wants to change. Everybody wants to have the experience of Enlightenment, the bliss of Enlightenment and the clarity of Enlightenment, but nobody really wants to change. They don't want to give up anything for that Enlightenment. Nobody wants to give up any of their strongly held beliefs or their future. It is precisely because of this that most people, in spite of having fantastic spiritual episodes, do not really change. If you want to be Free, you must become so intoxicated with the direct experience of the Absolute Truth that nothing could possibly remain the same.

Right Action

You Will See How Delicate It All Is

What Does It Mean to Be Serious?

You Have to Be Willing to Sacrifice Negative
Freedom

You Are Doing Exactly What You Want
to Be Doing

Your Whole Life Should Be a Clear Reflection
of What You Know to Be True

Right Action Is the End of Karma

You Will See How Delicate It All Is

When you realize the true significance of Enlightenment you will say, "Oh my God! This is so precious. This is it. This is the end of all seeking." This discovery is very subtle. Most people miss it because they're very gross-minded and therefore distracted.

If you look deeply you'll see why every move you make is so important. You will see how delicate it all is.

What Does It Mean to Be Serious?

Q: What does it mean to be serious?

A: Being serious means consistency and integrity of action. Being serious means you won't betray yourself or your deepest convictions. Most people betray themselves all the time. When you are truly serious you can no longer live a life made up of compromise and hypocrisy.

Many people assume that they are serious because they think that they want to be Free. It is only your behavior that expresses what you truly want, not what you think you want.

You Have to Be Willing to Sacrifice Negative Freedom

You have to be willing to sacrifice negative freedom if you want to be Awake.

Negative freedom is the freedom to be confused, the freedom to be vague, and the freedom to do just as you please. That kind of freedom must be sacrificed. It is only through conscious intention that you choose to identify with that which is other than Truth. Only when the absolute choice to be Awake is made can everything truly change. A tremendous sacrifice is made in making that choice because you have to sacrifice negative freedom.

You have to be willing to sacrifice negative freedom and fully embrace the bondage of Liberation if you want to be Awake. Very few people are interested in that.

You Are Doing Exactly What
You Want to Be Doing

Q: I have always thought of myself as a person who was very serious about spiritual matters. I never doubted that I wanted to be Free, but my experience shows me again and again that I must be fooling myself. This makes me think that I'm not as serious as I thought I was. This makes me think that maybe I don't know what I'm doing.

A: You always know what you are doing. Everyone knows exactly what they are doing.

Q: So why don't I change?

A: Because you are not yet ready to change. Because you have not yet truly embraced the urgency of the human condition. Many people, in spite of having had deep spiritual experiences, still do not become deadly serious. They allow themselves to continue to fool themselves. They allow themselves to continue to live in the illusion of ignorance and bondage.

Have no doubt that you are doing exactly what you want to be doing.

Your Whole Life Should Be a Clear Reflection of What You Know to Be True

Q: What has been plaguing me in my observations of my life is the pervasiveness of my hypocrisy. It drives me crazy. What I recognize as true never comes out, never leaves my lips.

A: What comes out of your mouth should be a clear reflection of what you know to be true. But not only that—your whole life should be a clear reflection of what you know to be true.

Q: When the outer is not a reflection of what I know to be true I feel like a hypocrite.

A: The point is, are you living what you know? There is a big gap between what most seekers claim to have experienced at one time or another and the life that they lead. If you can't live what you have experienced then you haven't realized it. If you truly have realized it then you *have* to live it. That is non-duality.

When you have truly woken up and found out who you are the inner and the outer should be one and the same.

Right Action Is the End of Karma

Q: Does fearlessness mean not being afraid of fear?

A: Yes, to be fearless means not being intimidated by fear. Not being intimidated by fear means whether you experience fear or not it can no longer have the power to prevent you from doing the right thing. When fear can no longer prevent you from doing the right thing it is living proof that you have won. Fear must not be able to frighten you to such a degree that it inhibits correct action. It is when we act that karma is created, and that is why action itself must be correct. The more you are able to do the right thing, the correct action, the more free you will know yourself to be.

Q: Are you saying that there are good and bad actions?

A: No, not good and bad actions. I'm speaking about right actions, or correct actions. That is the Enlightened action which is not motivated by fear or desire; that action which is not motivated by self-interest.

Enlightenment is the end. Realize that. Find it for yourself. That is as far as you have to go. If you realize that and stay there right action will be the result.

Destruction of Karma

Does Thought Create Karma?

When You Truly Pay Attention
Karma Comes to an End

Where All Karma Comes to an End

Nothing Left

How Can I Destroy Karma?

Does Thought Create Karma?

Q: Does thought create karma?

A: When there is belief in the reality of thought, then karma is going to be created. When there is absolutely no belief in the reality of thought then no karma can possibly be created.

It is only what you do or don't do that creates karma. If you understand this deeply then you will find that who you are has absolutely nothing to do with what you think.

When You Truly Pay Attention Karma Comes to an End

Q: Do you have to be careful about your thoughts?

A: Everyone has to be very careful about their thoughts. To be careful means to pay close attention, that's all. You have to be diligent. You must be mindful every second and between each and every second, otherwise you will definitely make a mistake.

Q: Is that a practice?

A: No, it's a way of life. If your desire for Enlightenment is sincere then mindfulness will be there naturally. It will be there because you won't want to get caught, because you won't want to get stuck, because you don't want to make a mistake. If your desire for Enlightenment is unconditional the kind of attention I'm speaking about will be your natural state. When you choose to allow yourself no other option, mindfulness is choiceless. With this kind of sincerity, when you look back over your shoulder you will find that there is nothing there.

When you truly pay attention, karma comes to an end.

Where All Karma Comes to an End

The holy life is the easiest life of all. That is because the holy life is a life of non-resistance. In the holy life you are effortlessly carried by the river in the current of Nirvana. Everybody else is struggling. Unnecessarily they are grabbing weeds, pulling themselves up on the shore of samsara. They get caught again and again along the bank in the weeds as you flow by, going downstream. Weeds appear on either side of you, beckoning you to grab onto them. If you do you will resist the current and when you resist the current moving downstream you will always suffer.

In the river it is always cool and refreshing. That's where all karma comes to an end. When this river takes you in its current you will be absolutely powerless.

At that fast speed, in that middle place, you know that there is absolutely nothing you can do to change anything or to control anything. Remain in the center of the river always. In the center you will always be swept along by the current. Swept along by the current, you cannot hold onto *anything*. When you can no longer hold onto any branch or the shore in any way, you are Free.

Nothing Left

Enlightenment is the end of history, the end of time and the end of becoming.

When you wake up from the dream, the dream is extinguished. In the perfect condition there is nothing left. All karma has been destroyed. Karma and the dream are one and the same. Waking up from the dream means realizing that nothing ever happened. With Enlightenment there is no history. It has been burned out of existence. Time itself has been destroyed.

In time there is continuity created by the desire to become. The desire to become creates continuity from one moment to another, from one day to another, from one week to another, from one month to another, from one year to another, and even from one lifetime to another. The desire to become creates a chain of cause and effect that leads us forward in time. The relationship between cause and effect, action and reaction, all arising out of the desire to become, builds up momentum. This momentum started somewhere, someplace a long time ago.

Imagine this momentum as a beam of light which has been traveling for millennia. This beam of light is time, is karma, is individuality. Enlightenment occurs when this beam of light meets a mirror that appears out of nowhere. When this mirror suddenly appears, the beam of light hits the mirror, is forced to go back on itself and is completely extinguished. The mirror erases its entire history.

What does this mean? This means that that which was real suddenly ceases to have ever existed. What was before no longer is. This means that it all, from the very beginning, suddenly never was. In one brief instant, that which had existed literally never happened.

This is the destruction of karma, and of time.

How Can I Destroy Karma?

Q: How can I destroy karma?

A: If you are truly interested in destroying karma then you have to be ready to disappear. If you want karma to disappear then you have to disappear and once disappeared you have to *stay* disappeared. As long as you are around there will always be karma. Karma is like a shadow. If you are not there then you cannot cast any shadow.

Vigilance

Doubt

If in the Face of Revelation You Allow
Yourself to Doubt

You Can Forget Everything in Less Than
One-Billionth of a Second

Doubt Has Nothing to Do with Discrimination

Don't Doubt

Will You Be Seduced by Maya?

Self-Doubt Is the Most Insidious Form of Doubt

If in the Face of Revelation
You Allow Yourself to Doubt

A human being can experience only an instant of transcendence and then spend the next thirty years thinking back to that one moment. In retrospect they know that nothing could ever come near the preciousness that was revealed to them in that brief instant. An entire lifetime can be spent knowing that that was the only time they were completely alive. Why did they lose touch with that experience? It was because of doubt.

When there is a profound revelation, in the very recognition that "this is revelation," you have to become serious about your own life. The instant you recognize that you are seeing the truth as it is, you must realize the implications of what is being revealed to you. If not betrayed even once then your confidence in that revelation can only grow. The stronger that confidence, the deeper will be your wisdom. But if in the face of that revelation you needlessly allow yourself to indulge in doubt, you begin to walk down a precarious road, because by doing so your confidence will be undermined.

It takes a long, long time to heal the mess of destructive indulgence in doubt in the face of potential Enlightenment.

You Can Forget Everything in Less Than One-Billionth of a Second

With doubt you have to be careful. You can forget everything in less than one-billionth of a second. Freedom has no history, so when the channel seems to switch and you feel like you are back in time, if your surrender isn't perfect you will have no memory of the Freedom you were just immersed in. It doesn't matter how long you were immersed in it, because it never was, the minute you are back in time.

If your surrender isn't perfect you will instantly get deluded again by time and thought, because you are dealing with a condition that has no history to it, and that is what is forgotten over and over and over again.

Doubt Has Nothing to Do with Discrimination

Q: I'm having a difficult time struggling with doubt.

A: If you want to be Free indulgence in and preoccupation with doubt can be very dangerous. Be very wary of doubt. Doubt is mechanically produced by the ego, and has nothing to do with discrimination. In most people the power of discrimination is very weak and underdeveloped, and it is only because of this that people ever get lost.

Q: How can I tell the difference between doubt and discrimination?

A: Discrimination makes you strong, doubt makes you weak. At times when your heart knows something is right, often the mind will doubt the heart. This can make progress very difficult. This delicate knowing of rightness has to be nurtured. The intimations of rightness are like little seeds that are just beginning to sprout. They need to be watered in order to grow. If you water these delicate intimations with doubt it is like pouring poison where you should be pouring water.

Don't Doubt

Q: The conditioning that I have grown up with sometimes clouds the path. It causes me to doubt my heart.

A: Do not doubt it.

Q: It's easy to say.

A: It is easy to say. It's also easy to do. That's why I say, "Don't doubt." As long as you doubt, you will keep losing touch with your heart.

Q: I'm not clear on how to get rid of the doubt.

A: By throwing it out. If you saw your child playing in the kitchen, noticed she had found a bottle of rat poison and could see she was about to drink it, what would you do?

Q: I would slap it out of her hand.

A: Yes. Because you know how dangerous it is. When you know how dangerous doubt is, you will do the same thing. An ignorant person doesn't realize how dangerous doubt is, so they allow themselves to indulge in doubt and by doing so they destroy the possibility of truly waking up in this birth.

Will You Be Seduced by Maya?

If you are not careful doubt will completely destroy any chance of Liberation for you in this life. Doubt is only an expression of Maya dancing around you, calling for your attention. All except the most astute, the most serious and the most dedicated will be swept away by the tide of Maya's deception. They will surely be tricked, fooled or sidetracked by this adversary that can be so extraordinarily deceptive.

If you want to be happy you have to be willing to fight for it. When the demons come and dance around you, the one who aspires to be Enlightened, trying to convince you to turn back from your quest, what will you do? Will you be seduced by them or not?

Self-Doubt Is the Most Insidious
Form of Doubt

Q: I have no doubt about the Absolute Reality but I have doubt about my ability to realize it completely.

A: If it's true that you have no doubt about the Absolute Reality, then it would not be possible for you to have any doubt about your own ability to realize it. Having no doubt about the Absolute Reality *is* the realization of it.

Self-doubt is the most insidious form of doubt. It's just another form of temptation. Many people get foiled by it. They use self-doubt as an excuse to keep making the same mistakes. What is self-doubt? It's only an excuse not to change.

Pride and Humility

The Only Appropriate Response to Freedom
Is Humility

When Profound Humility Is Present

Real Confidence in the Truth Only Comes from
True Knowledge of Emptiness

Pride Is Vicious

The Only Appropriate Response to Freedom Is Humility

Q: I have been experiencing a lot of freedom lately and at the same time I also recognize that there arises a tendency to create ownership of that freedom.

A: This is pride. The only appropriate response to the experience of Freedom is humility. There is no other appropriate response. Any other response to the experience of Freedom than perfect humility is a demonstration of ignorance and indicates a very shallow level of understanding.

In the true recognition of real Freedom there isn't anybody left to own anything. Most people never look deeply enough into their own experience to find this out for themselves and it is because of this that they get into trouble.

When the need to own any insight or revelation no longer arises — this is a sign that humility has been won.

When Profound Humility Is Present

The deeper the humility that a human being
is endowed with the more profound will be their
Enlightenment. The more genuine humility there is in
a human being the deeper the impact the initial experience of Enlightenment is going to have. People who are
very proud may have powerful experiences but the
understanding that results from those experiences will
be short-lived. A proud person will soon be left with
only a memory of the great event. When profound
humility is present the transformation will remain, and
that human being's behavior will demonstrate something
very precious and rare. You will be able to recognize it
in their tone of voice, the choice of their words, the way
they move their body and the look in their eyes.

Real Confidence in the Truth Only Comes from True Knowledge of Emptiness

Q: How can one tell when a human being has indeed realized the Truth? What are the signs of that realization in human behavior that one can look for?

A: Confidence in deep realization of the Truth is always expressed as profound humility — and profound humility can only arise from a true knowledge of emptiness. This happens only when a person has realized that emptiness as none other than their own Self. This cannot happen if a person has only experienced or recognized emptiness once or twice. Only when emptiness has been deeply realized will profound humility be a natural and spontaneous reflection of that realization.

When a person only thinks they know something, they are arrogant. But when a person knows they know something, that is a very different matter.

Pride Is Vicious

Pride is vicious. Pride is the most vicious enemy for those who claim they want to be Enlightened in this birth. If you want to be Enlightened in this birth then give pride the highest priority for your attention, because pride is one of the most difficult obstacles to Enlightenment.

Equate pride with whatever you imagine ego to be. Pride and ego are the same thing. Pride is the enemy if you want to be Free because it is pride that causes you to betray your deepest longing for Liberation.

Pride has a very ugly face. Pride is based on the idea that you know something. When you think you know something you feel special, and when you feel special you are separate. Ideas of specialness or superiority will separate you from what you claim to want the most. As long as there are any ideas, gross or subtle, of specialness that are being cherished, you are sowing the very same seeds of violence and aggression that the whole human race is lost in.

Even for those who are Enlightened pride is a difficult obstacle to perfection.

You Will Be Tested

You Will Be Tested

A Rare Human Being

You Have to Be Willing to Fight for It

Be Like a Strong Tree That Can't Be Moved

It Is Possible to Be Tempted

It Is Difficult for Most People to Sustain
That Perfect Condition

How Can I Find the Courage to Live Fully
What I Have Realized?

How Can I Not Get Lost Again?

Stay Always Where Your Deepest
Understanding Is

You Will Be Tested

We are all tested. Anybody who is so bold as to accept Enlightenment here and now in this life will be tested even more.

The Enlightened person threatens the status quo. The way they think and the way they speak is very threatening to the corrupt world we live in. The living fact of Enlightenment makes people uneasy, frightened and angry.

Anyone who is so bold as to accept Enlightenment in this life will be very severely tested. They will have to face all kinds of trouble.

A Rare Human Being

Q: If someone is fully Enlightened, would it still be possible for them to avoid facing difficult and unpleasant aspects of their own personality? Would it still be possible for them to avoid facing difficult situations outside themselves that need to be faced?

A: One definition of fully Enlightened is that the capacity to avoid is gone. If someone is fully Enlightened, they no longer possess the ability to deceive themselves the way most people do. Everything is faced choicelessly, pleasant or unpleasant. Most people are very resistant to the possibility of facing everything in this way.

Q: It seems that denial or avoidance is actually what creates a separate identity.

A: Yes, precisely. That's all a separate identity is. When there is no longer any denial or avoidance, you will be a Liberated human being.

Only a rare human being has the capacity to face everything as it is without hesitation, without fear, without preconditions and without worry.

You Have to Be Willing to Fight for It

If you dare to take up the banner of Enlightenment you will be attacked from all sides. From the inside you will be attacked by your own mind and from the outside you will be attacked by everyone else's mind. Anyone who dares to succeed automatically presents a huge threat. If true Freedom is going to survive within you, you have to be willing to fight for it. You have to have a sword in each hand at all times. One sword is for your own mind and the other sword is for everyone else's mind. You must be ready to use them.

Anyone who wants to be truly Free must be willing to stand alone in the Truth.

Be Like a Strong Tree That Can't Be Moved

Q: I'm not sure of my own strength or my own fortitude. I'm not sure if I have what it takes to be Enlightened.

A: You have to make up your mind once and for all and you have to be deadly serious about it. Most people allow themselves to keep changing their minds. When you keep changing your mind about this you allow yourself to tamper with something that should not be tampered with. When that which is most precious and unthinkably sacred has been set in place you should let it be. If you tamper with it, it is like tampering with the roots of a very young tree. If you want a young tree to grow big and strong you need to leave the roots alone. If you keep uprooting the tree from the earth and then putting it back in again, you will weaken the tree.

When you dare to hold up the banner of Enlightenment you are sure to experience the consequences of your own actions in a more profound manner than you would ordinarily. You must be ready to face and accept the consequences of taking a stand in the Absolute. You must be firmly rooted in that. You must be ready. If you are not, yet take that stand anyway, the consequences will blow you all over the place, like a twig in the middle of a hurricane.

Be like a strong tree that can't be moved.

It Is Possible to Be Tempted

We can be tempted by so many things inside of ourselves and outside of ourselves. This is why it is so important that our interest must be in Freedom alone. Many people think that after they have realized who they are, it would be impossible for them to go back to the old way of being. They think that it would be impossible to be tempted by their old way of seeing. Even after Realization it is shockingly easy for people to slip right back into old ways of seeing and being without even realizing that they have done so. That's why you have to be very careful. Realize choicelessness and you will be careful.

It Is Difficult for Most People to Sustain That Perfect Condition

It is difficult for most people to sustain that perfect condition that is experienced in profound realization. Perfect purity and perfect innocence that are the gift of grace are in most cases soon lost due to the temptation to be somebody once again. In time the desire to be somebody slowly creeps back. Most people don't realize it when it's happening. This craving to be special poisons the innocence that is born out of the realization of emptiness and because of that, the purity of that realization is polluted.

How Can I Find the Courage to Live Fully What I Have Realized?

Q: How can I find the courage to live fully what I have realized?

A: When you have seen the truth for yourself and you have consciously recognized and acknowledged that fact, everything changes. Prior to this recognition, you could always say, "I didn't know any better." After this recognition, you always do know better. Whether you choose to act like you do know better or not is another matter. But from the moment you have recognized the truth yourself you actually no longer have an excuse for not knowing it.

When there has been a conscious acknowledgement of a realization of the truth, then there is responsibility. Some people acknowledge that responsibility and act accordingly. Most do not.

Where do you find the courage to live fully what you have realized? From your own realization, that's where. The truth itself is what will give you the courage. The truth of your own experience, which you yourself have recognized, will alone give you all the courage you will ever need.

How Can I Not Get Lost Again?

Q: Once I have glimpsed the truth, how can I maintain that vision and not get lost again?

A: By having faith, love and devotion for that which the mind cannot grasp. This takes a great deal of courage, because the mind will try to pollute anything and everything. Even the most sublime realization, the mind will try to corrupt, taint and destroy. This is not the mind's fault. It can't help it. It doesn't know how to do anything else. Unfortunately, most people unwittingly participate in this process. It is because of this that they get lost again and again.

Q: Does the mind ever come to terms with that which it cannot grasp?

A: No, the mind never does, but *you* can. When you realize that you are completely helpless before the truth then you will automatically discover that the mind is also helpless before the truth. That discovery is Liberation.

Stay Always Where Your Deepest Understanding Is

Once you have taken that leap, the only thing that is important is that you do not allow yourself to slip back. When you have seen the truth deeply for yourself and you have no doubt about it, it is very important that you do not allow yourself to slip back from what you have realized. Stay always where your deepest understanding is. Do not allow any space to grow between your own deepest realization and the life that you live.

It may require great diligence to stay in that which is new.

When Your Boat Hits the Shore
(Meditations on the End of Seeking)

When Your Boat Hits the Shore

Leave All Experiences Behind

When You Wake Up You No Longer Feel
That You Are Moving Anywhere

When Your Boat Hits the Shore

If we want to find Reality we must seek for it, but the instant that that Reality starts to reveal itself we should cease to make effort. When our seeking has been fruitful, and the intimations of that which we have been searching for start to dawn on us, all effort and control must be abandoned so that we can be available to perceive directly the very thing we have been searching for. Rowing in a boat from the ocean to the shore when our boat arrives at its destination it is imperative that we get out of the boat. The boat represents all our ideas, our effort, our striving and our fears. The shore is the unknown.

For most people the unconditional acceptance of the totality of the Truth as it is poses an unbearable threat in the face of which they are terrified. For this reason most individuals even long after their boat has touched the sand of yonder shore prefer the familiarity of the boat rather than accepting the perfect Freedom of abandoning all reference points whatsoever and jumping out of the boat and into the unknown forever.

Leave All Experiences Behind

Spiritual experiences can set you Free, but they can also entrap you. You have to find the confidence to leave all experiences behind you. The deeper you dive into the Truth all experiences will start to fade. Something else will begin to occupy you that has nothing to do with time, and has nothing to do with any event that could ever take place in time.

When You Wake Up You No Longer Feel That You Are Moving Anywhere

People go through their lives thinking that they are going somewhere. From morning to night, from birth to death, they think they are going somewhere. That is part of the great illusion. When you wake up you no longer feel that you are going anywhere. You can see that you have stopped moving and you realize that the whole world and everyone in it has fallen away from you. You have discovered that you are at the very center of the universe. When this happens the intelligent person doesn't move, they only watch and see what happens. If they can resist the temptation to move, nothing will change ever again.

Enlightenment
Is Not a
Personal Matter

Compassion and Service

Compassion

Enlightenment Is Not Something You Can
Do Anything With

Self-Realization Is Evolution

Compassion

Q: In the search for and discovery of Enlightenment, where does compassion come in?

A: Ideally in a place that you will know absolutely nothing about. Many people are very ambitious. They want to be owners of this most precious virtue. They are very busy trying to cultivate it. Compassion is the natural and spontaneous result of Liberation. Enlightened compassion is owned by nobody and the compassionate one knows nothing about compassion. This kind of compassion is very powerful. It has nothing to do with ideas.

If you want to be Enlightened forget about compassion. If you are up to it, seek Enlightenment. If you know you are not up to it, then help. Help all the suffering people in the world in a practical way. There is so much to be done. Either do something to help other people in a practical way or forget about everybody and seek Enlightenment. Do you understand? Do one or do the other. Stop thinking about compassion and start *doing* something for others or forget about everyone and Realize the source of all compassion.

Enlightenment Is Not Something You Can Do Anything With

Q: What can you do with Enlightenment in terms of service and helping others?

A: You can be yourself. The most delicate and difficult task possible to accomplish in this life is simply to *be Free*. One who succeeds is very rare. It is hardly ever seen. If a person can *be* Free, it is the greatest blessing. It means an alternative to the human mess is possible. Simply being awake and staying awake is a demonstration of the solution. Living Freedom *is* the solution. You become the answer. You become the solution. It's very rare. Few have the courage to do it.

Q: But what about compassion and the suffering of other people?

A: Enlightenment is not something you can do anything with. If Enlightenment is real it will possess you. After that what will happen will happen but you won't know how it happened.

Self-Realization Is Evolution

Q: Considering how much violence and suffering there is in the world, seeking for my own Freedom on a spiritual journey seems like a very selfish endeavor.

A: Nothing could be further from the truth. You are doing the human race the highest service by Realizing your Self. Self-Realization is evolution. Coming to the end of aggressive, destructive and selfish behavior is evolution in action. When you evolve to the point that you are able to actively manifest the profound understanding discovered in Self-Realization you are cooperating with all the forces of nature. Only then will your own life be the very expression of the opposite of everything you claim to abhor. What more can you possibly do? What more can anybody possibly do than that? When you have Realized your Self you simply *are*. When you have found that harmony that you are, then you will be that harmony and no longer an obstruction to it. When struggle has come to an end, so does all division.

Enlightenment Is Not
a Personal Matter

Enlightenment Is Not a Personal Matter

Recognition of the Truth Is the Discovery
of True Conscience

The Reason for All Spiritual Experience
Is Evolution

Can We Take This Next Step?

Enlightenment Is Not a Personal Matter

When you think about Enlightenment, it is important that you include other people in that idea.

Transcendence will be yours when you begin to accept responsibility for the condition of the whole human race. When you give yourself up in unconditional surrender, automatically you rise up beyond the very limited perspective that most of the human race remains forever lost in. You come upon an infinitely greater perspective in which all questions disappear.

The by-product of Enlightenment is that you cease to suffer the way you suffered in the past. But the most important benefit is for the whole race. Why? *Because someone actually will have stopped.* When this happens, there is an explosive reaction that is magnetic.

If you feel disturbed by all the conflict and suffering that you see in the world but are unwilling to come to the end of conflict within yourself, then you can be sure that you are not serious.

Recognition of the Truth Is
the Discovery of True Conscience

Q: What creates the kind of stability that allows a sublime realization to remain uncorrupted?

A: Clarity of intention creates stability. That means clearly knowing that you want to be free more than anything else.

Q: Even the best of intentions often become corrupted. It seems so difficult.

A: Yes, that's true. Often when people have sublime experiences, because their intention to be free is not absolutely clear, the experiences soon become only inspiring memories. The basic structure of the ego usually remains intact and fundamentally unchanged. But after such an experience, they will always know that there is another possibility. They will know this from their own experience because they will have realized it themselves and the memory of that experience will haunt them.

Q: Why will they be haunted?

271

A: Because a recognition of the truth is the discovery of true conscience. Being haunted by the truth is being haunted by your own true conscience. The point of these experiences is for you to realize what your part in the big drama of life is. Most people are so concerned only with themselves that they do not feel any responsibility for anyone else. The more deeply a person has realized, the deeper will be the birth of the kind of conscience I am speaking about. In profound realization, it is possible to come upon a perspective that is so vast that you will suddenly feel overwhelmed by the tremendous responsibility that you have simply being a human being. You will recognize how important your own life truly is.

The Reason for All Spiritual Experience Is Evolution

The mess of the human condition is that fundamental trust has not yet been realized. The true value of profound spiritual experience lies in the discovery of that fundamental trust.

The full realization of Enlightenment is the evolutionary leap to which all spiritual experiences ultimately lead. In deep spiritual experience a human being realizes that which is impersonal. In that realization a profound trust is found. In the discovery of that trust it is possible for a human being to liberate him or herself from tendencies toward aggression and permanently destroy the illusion of separation that those tendencies arise from. The result of this discovery is a level of integrity that is deep and profound and which manifests consistently at all levels of human expression. If the evolutionary leap is to take place then the final outcome of true spiritual experience *must* result in this kind of purity.

Spiritual experiences and their results are not meant for the individual. They are for the evolution of the whole race.

Can We Take This Next Step?

Can human beings trust each other and in that trust abide together harmoniously? History would tell us that mankind has not done that well. The point of all spiritual experience is to bring a human being to the point where he or she can be a social creature who is able to live with other human beings in a non-aggressive manner.

Looking very objectively the spiritual journey is more practical than esoteric.

The death of the individual is the birth of this evolutionary leap. Can we take this next step? It's up to each and every individual as long as they understand that they have nothing to gain from it.

Glossary

Dharma: Truth.

Karma: The consequences of action motivated
by ignorance.

Maya: Illusion; the way things *appear* to be.

Nirvana: The bliss of the conscious knowing
of Liberation.

Sadhana: Spiritual practice.

Samsara: The endless cycle of suffering generated
as a result of karma.

Index

For more information about Andrew Cohen and his teaching please contact:

Moksha Foundation
P.O. Box 5265
Larkspur, CA 94977
USA
tel: 415-256-9063
fax: 415-256-9160

FACE Centre (Friends of Andrew Cohen in Europe)
Centre Studios
Englands Lane
London NW3 4YD
UK
tel: 44-171-483-3732
fax: 44-171-916-3170